The Celeb

DIARIES

THE SENSATIONAL INSIDE STORY OF THE CELEBRITY DECADE

MARK FRITH

EBURY
PRESS

Mark Frith took the helm at *Heat* in early 2000 and increased sales from 65,000 to over 550,000. He has won every major British publishing award in the process, including PPA Editor of the Year twice and, in 2005, the BSME Mark Boxer Award for special achievement in UK magazine publishing. Prior to *Heat* he was editor of *Smash Hits* and *Sky Magazine*. He has also presented BBC TV's *Liquid News*. He resigned from *Heat* in February 2008 in order to write this book.

3 5 7 9 10 8 6 4 2

First published in 2008 by Ebury Press, an imprint of Ebury Publishing
A Random House Group company
This edition published 2009

Copyright © Mark Frith 2008

Mark Frith has asserted his right to be identified as the author of this
Work in accordance with the Copyright, Designs and Patents Act 1988

The Random House Group Limited Reg. No. 954009

Addresses for companies within the Random House Group
can be found at www.randomhouse.co.uk

A CIP catalogue record for this book is
available from the British Library

The Random House Group Limited supports The Forest
Stewardship Council (FSC), the leading international forest
certification organisation. All our titles that are printed on Greenpeace
approved FSC certified paper carry the FSC logo. Our paper
procurement policy can be found at www.rbooks.co.uk/environment

Printed in the UK by CPI Cox & Wyman, Reading, RG1 8EX

ISBN 9780091928094

To buy books by your favourite authors and register for offers visit
www.rbooks.co.uk

To Victoria Beckham, who saved *Heat* magazine.

And probably now really regrets it.

Contents

Introduction

Celebrities. I've been writing about them for eight years solid and I still don't understand them. I often would have meetings with the *Heat* team that would end with me shaking my head and saying the words, 'They're all MAD! The lot of them!' There is no group of people on God's earth more infuriating, ego-driven, contradictory, pampered, spoilt and downright ridiculous than celebrities. And for eight years I was caught up in their madness.

When I was a kid, magazines – and the people in them – were the centre of my life. I'd buy four or five a week, subsidised (although only just) by the worst-paid paper round in Sheffield (£2.50 a week for five morning shifts. I'm not joking!) There's just something about magazines. They were everything to me. My favourite was *Smash Hits* and I cherished every single page: pored over each one, consumed every word, examined every picture before turning the page and getting upset cos that meant I was two pages nearer the end. I loved that they were produced by people who were passionate about their subject. I loved how the journalists who wrote for them crafted each sentence with skill and humour. On my paper round I'd dawdle as I read all the magazines (and the *Sun*'s gossip column) in such detail that the good people of Woodseats in Sheffield would either get the wrong paper or the right one far too late. I became obsessed. I read everything: free newspapers, leaflets on buses, my grandma's copy of *Woman's Own* magazine, *everything*.

I never, as a painfully shy lad growing up in Yorkshire, *ever* thought I would actually get to work at a magazine. Why ever would I? And anyway, I was too shy to speak to anyone so there were practical problems there. The careers teacher at my rough comprehensive school told me only out-going people became journalists.

But still, I told everyone who asked that I was going to work for a magazine one day. They didn't believe it and I didn't believe it but I didn't have any better answers. For five years, from the age of 13 to 18, I kept telling people I was going to work at a magazine but did absolutely nothing about it. Then, in autumn 1988 during my first week at the Polytechnic Of East London, I plucked up the courage to go along to the offices of the Student Union magazine, asked them if they wanted a pop music column and they said they did. My confidence gradually increased: I ended up editing it and then one day, in the launderette, I saw an advert for a job at *Smash Hits* ...

I loved working at a pop magazine. Music was my thing and it was easy for me to write about it. *Smash Hits* led to *Sky* magazine and I was suddenly reliving my student magazine days doing a magazine for hedonistic (or pretend hedonistic) college kids. Then, in autumn 1997, I was approached about a new magazine, *Heat*, that was being lined up for launch. *Heat* magazine was intended to be a serious, wordy look at the world of entertainment.

We launched with a huge fanfare on 1 February 1999. We knew by week three that *Heat* had flopped. Big time. Why? Good question. It wasn't a bad magazine but it was probably the wrong magazine. That year, 1999, was all about Posh and Becks' wedding and Posh and Becks' wedding was all about gossip, glamour and fashion. Those were the three reasons this event was interesting, but also there were other famous people out there who were becoming interesting for similar reasons. In spring 2000, the publishers Emap relaunched *Heat* as a magazine about these celebrities, with me in charge. This book begins as I'm handed the reins and hurtles through a time when celebrity got bigger, more democratic and a lot more controversial. It's one hell of a roller coaster ride.

Originally I never wanted to do magazines about 'celebrities', as music magazines were my thing, but somehow I ended up doing this. And, as people took me into their confidence, allowed me in the dressing rooms or photo studios or parties, I saw the madness of it all at close hand. And it fascinated me – I'm intrigued by how people relate to each other, how they fall for each other and fall out. The world of celebrity is the new human zoo and I loved watching it all.

I'm very proud of the fact that I managed to not get sucked in by it, to take it seriously or believe *I* was famous simply because I wrote about famous people. None of these famous people you read about here became my friends. I do happen to have two friends that are quite famous but I only know them because my girlfriend went to school with them. I promised them I wouldn't mention either in the book (they're both really boring anyway).

So why do the book? I, more than perhaps anyone else, have had a front-row seat for the celebrity decade. I wanted to document that. I can't deny I was inspired by Piers Morgan's brilliant book *The Insider* because I was. I read it on holiday in the summer of 2005 and thought to myself that one day I'd document my time at a magazine in the way he documented his time at a newspaper, never thinking I'd actually get a chance to do it. But, as you'll see from reading the book, my attitude to life is pretty different to his and the magazine world is a completely different environment from the newspaper world: far less brutal, far more relaxed (a little too relaxed at times). Like him I made mistakes – including one doozy in late 2007 – but when you have to make hundreds of different decisions a week you don't get everything right.

So, this *is* the story of The Celebrity Decade, as it will come to be known, told by a lad from Yorkshire watching it all from close quarters. But it's also the story of a magazine: the people who graced its pages and the characters who created it. Cos magazines are great.

Three days before I wrote this introduction I was in a newsagent's near my home with my two-year-old son. He likes our newsagent's for two very good reasons. Firstly it has three steps leading up to it and he loves climbing steps. Secondly the newsagent's has magazines in it. So, on Sunday he climbed the steps and ran – ran! – over to where the kids' magazines were, handily laid out at kid height. There he surveyed the scene, spied the *Teletubbies* magazine and pulled it out of the selection. 'Okay, you can have it. But I need to take it over to the man because I have to pay for it.' I try and take it out of his hand but he gives it a short tug towards him. 'Danny ...' He starts sobbing. 'I need to ...' He isn't letting go. 'All right!'

I wander over to the counter, without the magazine, and explain to them what's happening.

'Hi, sorry, my son has a magazine that I'd like to pay for. It's £1.99, can I just give you the money for it now, because he won't let me bring it to the counter and ...' As I say the word 'he' I look down to see my son. He is lying on the floor, painstakingly examining every bit of the opening page of the magazine before turning the page and doing the same again on the next one.

Like I say, there's just something about magazines ...

Prologue

I've done some pretty stupid things in my time editing this magazine, but this has to be the most stupid.

In fact, I can't believe we're going to go through with this.

It's 4 p.m., Wednesday afternoon. In three days' time the biggest celebrity wedding since Posh and Becks takes place. Cheryl Tweedy, Girls Aloud's feisty, mouthy ex-reality TV star and singer, is marrying one of the richest young men in Britain: England and Chelsea footballer Ashley Cole. It's a huge wedding and like all huge weddings it has been bought up, exclusively, by ... *OK* magazine.

The all-important preparations are being made over the next few days. Us cheeky kids from *Heat* are not allowed in, naturally.

So I've told the team that we're going to gatecrash.

Publicly *Heat* magazine, because we're cooler than all the other celeb mags, hates the whole magazine wedding thing. I, Lucie, Hannah, Julian and the gang give endless interviews to celebrity 'talking heads' TV shows about how cheesy we think these weddings are, how sad we think it is that someone's big day is sullied by security guards who frisk you wherever you go and confiscate your cameras, about how really it's just about money and nothing to do with love and commitment and tradition.

In private, of course, we're all obsessed by the spectacle and I'm sure some of the *Heat* staff would love to work as part of a celebrity wedding reporting team.

So, what we attempt to do on our pages is to get the story behind the event. Find out what really happens behind the scenes.

I'll admit it, we do face a few problems when we attempt to cover a wedding we have no access to.

We have no pictures of the dress.

We have no pictures of the ceremony.

We won't be able to run an interview with the happy couple.

The other disadvantage we have (and this is a biggie) is that we have to print the magazine before the actual wedding happens. But look as though we've printed it after it happened. Yes, I know what you're thinking: 'That's ridiculous.' You're right, of course.

It's especially a problem if, say, you don't even know where the wedding is.

And we don't.

We need to find out where it is – and quickly. There's only one man for the job. Unfortunately he is unavailable, so we're sending Daniel Fulvio instead ...

How to explain Daniel Fulvio? He's in his early twenties, eccentric, laughs all the time, is nervous around authority but at other times (especially when he's had a drink) is the life and soul of the party. He's hard-working, intense and one hell of a character. And now he's been given the challenge of his career so far: to infiltrate the preparations for Cheryl Tweedy and Ashley Cole's wedding. He mustn't fail.

So, we know that Dan will be out of the office tomorrow roaming the countryside trying to find this wedding. But as we leave the office for the evening we're not quite sure which direction he'll be heading in.

Then, late this evening, my phone buzzed with a text. It's Dan. He's certain he knows where the wedding will be.

'Mark, heard it from several good sources that it's Highclere House in Berkshire. Off there first thing tomorrow morning. Over and out.'

Here we go.

Thursday 13 July

I get to the office at 9 as usual. Hannah's already in, working hard at it.

'He's got a hangover.'

'Who's got a hangover?'

'La Fulvio!'

She's laughing now. Good start – but he'll be fine.

He calls us from Paddington station. He's waiting for a train to Newbury (the nearest station to the hotel) and – because time is tight – he's trying to stand-up his hunch on his way over there.

'So I called them and tried to do my best premiership football-player voice to the girl who answered. I said, "I'm coming to Cheryl and Ashley's wedding this Saturday and I've just received the invite. Could you give me directions?" I could hear the guy speak to someone else. "I've got a guy on the phone asking about Cheryl and Ashley's wedding. What should I tell him?" That confirms it! I'm sure we've got the place!'

I'm really not so sure the phone call told us anything but he seems convinced. Anyway, time's running out. We've got to go for this.

An hour or so later we get another call. He's arrived. And there's a huge white marquee in the centre of the hotel's grounds.

BINGO!

Dan spies vans unloading stuff into the marquee – then follows the staff as they carry stuff out of them. Despite wearing a fluorescent green T-shirt with Tinkabelle performing a strip tease on it, Dan manages to fool the team into believing that he's an event-organiser.

Bloody hell. He's in!

The phone calls keep coming, each one more clandestine and in more hushed tones than the last.

'This tent is vast. It's huge – the size of a football pitch – and a dozen men are busy unpacking boxes and sound-testing a DJ box – pumping eardrum-shattering dance music. There is dry ice and a massive lighting rig. Wa-hey!'

Fulvio gets very excited at times. He raises his voice at the end of the call; he can't help himself.

His final sentence is triumphant.

They're preparing for the wedding reception of the century in here!'

I listen in as Hannah tries to get him off the line.

'Be careful,' she shouts down the phone. 'Call me again when you can.'

The next time we hear from him is 20 minutes later. He's since been chucked out of the main marquee by the person testing the sound – noooo!

Hmm, maybe that T-shirt he's wearing was a give-away. Memo to self: put a LOT more thought into the journalist's outfit next time (if there ever is a next time. Not sure my nerves can cope with this).

Anyway, then he went into the kitchens. He got chucked out of there too ...

The phone rings again. 'A woman with a clipboard saw me go in. I told her I was Cheryl's PA and that I was there to make sure everything was going according to plan for Saturday. She exchanged glances with this woman next to her and told me I'd need to speak to Cheryl about all of that.'

He's still not got anything that really stands up, of course, but we are beginning to banish any doubts we've had.

Because of the rumours we've heard, because of the marquee (and the sheer size of the thing), because of their attempts to chuck us out we are now convinced this is the place.

As editor, I have to make a decision and dramatically swing into action.

'Russ, we need some aerial shots of Highclere House as soon as possible – first thing tomorrow by the latest. Great epic shots showing the house and the marquee. It's huge, we really need to get the size and the scale of this event on to the page.'

We've asked Dan to look around a bit more – so he does. He checks out the portaloos and finds a tiny ornate chapel the house has onsite. That's where the ceremony will take place, of course! This all adds up perfectly. Making notes all the time he now has everything he needs: pages and pages of information.

This will be great. A proper news story. And it will look brilliant. I call him again.

'Dan, you can come back to the office. We've got the perfect piece. I can see it now – BEHIND THE SCENES AT THE CELEBRITY WEDDING OF THE DECADE!'

Today was a great day.

Friday 14 July

By lunchtime the feature is complete. The aerial shots of the venue look incredible, we've loads of information – everything from what food they'll be eating to the fact that in the men's portaloos the soap is black pepper and ginseng while in the ladies' it's mandarin and grapefruit. It's a proper news job.

However, at just after three, less than two hours before we finish work for the week, Hannah receives a troubling phone call.

A paparazzi photographer friend of hers tells her there's a lot of movement near a venue called Wrotham Park in Hertfordshire.

A convoy of cars with blacked-out windows has just sped into the grounds and other paps are on their way. They think Ashley Cole is in one of the cars. I call Dan over to my desk and let him know.

Dan – his face now as white as a sheet – phones Wrotham Park up. 'They say there's no wedding taking place this weekend.'

'Well, they would, wouldn't they!' I say.

'Yes. I guess.'

At just after five o'clock Deputy News Editor Charlotte gets a call from a showbiz reporter contact at the *Sun* saying that he's received an inventory and schedule detailing all the plans of the big day and that it is happening at ... yep, Wrotham Park.

Hannah holds her head in her hands.

'I saw the DJ set up, the food being prepared,' stammers Dan. 'The staff even admitted it.'

'Dan. Did anyone actually say to you that this was the venue of Cheryl's wedding?'

'No. But I mentioned her name to two different people and they didn't bat an eyelid when I did. They didn't flinch. Except ...'

'Go on?'

'The woman in the kitchens did give another woman a funny look.'

'So if this wasn't Cheryl and Ashley's wedding, what was it?'

'That's the thing! It was a wedding. It was huge and posh and DJs were setting up.'

I raise my voice.

'Are we *really* to believe that this whole event at Highclere House has been arranged just to put *us* off the scent. It must have cost a fortune! The marquee, all that food. That's the bit I don't get!'

Come on, Mark. What to do? I've summoned Al, our Creative Director, back from the pub. All mentions of Highclere House have now been stripped out and we've kept the copy as vague as possible. I've no idea what else we can do.

It's not a great piece but it's a piece. No one will die if we get it wrong (except perhaps Dan).

But I have to face facts. This is a disaster. A total cock up. *Heat* magazine, the most talked-about magazine of the last ten years, the one that transformed itself from Britain's biggest flop to an award-winning, world-famous, magazine-publishing sensation has just infiltrated THE WRONG BLOODY WEDDING.

Or even, possibly, not a wedding at all.

Dan feels terrible but it's as much my fault.

We all so much wanted to believe that we'd spoilt *OK*'s big exclusive of the year.

'Don't worry,' I say as he heads out of the office. 'You'll look back at this and laugh. One day.'

Saturday 15 July

This morning is like waking up with a hangover. I'm trying to piece together the events of yesterday by reading through the newspapers and surfing the web.

Here's what I can make out:

1. Highclere House *was* the original venue for the Cole/Tweedy wedding but they cancelled it months ago.
2. To protect *OK*'s exclusive the organisers decided Highclere may be a good decoy so they asked the venue not to deny the event was happening – which explains why the team were like they were with Dan.
3. What Dan infiltrated was a corporate event, bizarrely, not a wedding. That event is already over – the marquee is being dismantled this morning.
4. The actual Cole/Tweedy wedding ceremony has already taken place – it was yesterday.
5. The reception and party take place today – at Wrotham Park.
6. We've been had – good and proper.

It was never meant to be like this. When I was starting out in magazines it was all very straightforward. Pop group releases record. Record gets to number one. Keen, young reporter goes along and interviews said pop group. Interview gets written up. People read it.

Somehow, I've ended up in a position where I'm asking journalists to break into people's weddings, getting screamed at down the phone by TV presenters, printing half-naked pictures of the Prime Minister and nearly getting run over by film stars. How the hell did I get here?

Welcome to the life a celebrity magazine editor. Trust me, there's never a dull moment.

PART ONE
Hot

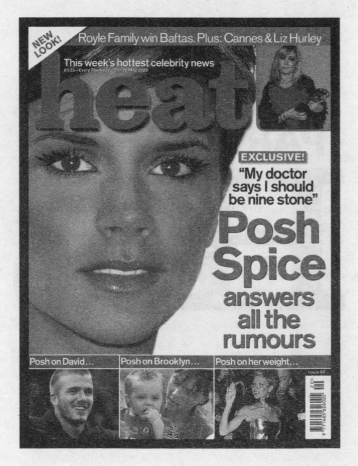

NEW LOOK!

Royle Family win Baftas. Plus: Cannes & Liz Hurley

This week's hottest celebrity news
£1.25 • Every Thursday • 20 – 26 May 2000

heat

EXCLUSIVE!

"My doctor says I should be nine stone"

Posh Spice
answers all the rumours

Posh on David...

Posh on Brooklyn...

Posh on her weight...

Issue 66

CHAPTER ONE
Posh to the rescue!
December 1999 – May 2000

Wednesday 8 December

I couldn't get home fast enough tonight. It's been a really mad day. I've got a lot of thinking to do. It all started with a very odd lunch.

Sue Hawken has been my boss for the majority of my adult life. And I was summoned to see her at short notice. Great, I thought, that'll be more bad news.

I sat in Bertorelli's on Frith Street in Soho playing with the breadsticks, wondering, to be honest, if she might be about to fire me. It's all been going so badly recently.

Heat – this bloody magazine I am meant to be editing – is the biggest (and most public) flop in the history of British magazines. We launched on 1 February as a smart, serious, wordy entertainment magazine aimed mostly at men. To say it hasn't gone well would be an understatement. It's been a disaster. We put out 300,000 copies of the first issue and sold about 70,000 of them. Since then things have gone from bad to worse. Now we're only selling half of that.

It doesn't help that I'm listed in the magazine as Editor but I'm not actually in charge. For the last year I've always had an Editorial Director above me and I've played deputy. Of course *I* want to run this magazine. I've got loads of ideas, enthusiasm and I just want my chance. But today, as I wait for Sue to arrive at the restaurant, it dawns on me that the game is probably up. It's over. They're going to fire me.

Sue arrives. Short, smartly dressed but serious to the point of scary, Sue Hawken has always frightened the life out of me: a foot shorter she may be but her blunt manner can bring me and anyone down to size. She's also not one for small talk. She sits down, asks me how things are going with the magazine and I automatically launch fully into defensive mode. I tell her about how the bad sales have affected me – the virtually sleepless nights, three in the last week – how I have a vision of the magazine that isn't getting through, about what *Heat* could be and what needs to be done.

'I understand that it's been rotten. It hasn't *exactly* been a barrel of laughs for the board either,' was her response.

A fair comment I suppose. Is this it then? Is this the moment she fires me? If she is going to do it she'll do it straightaway: no fanfare, no build-up, straight in there.

She opens the bottle of mineral water and pours herself a glass.

'I've got something to tell you, Mark.'

My mouth goes completely dry. I looked her in the eye (not something I find easy at the best of times, but being confronted with the big boss? Bloody terrifying!)

'David Davies is moving off *Heat*.'

I'm not being fired! Thank God. Come on, Mark, compose yourself.

'Oh. Right.'

'We want you to be in charge. Properly this time. But the magazine needs radical change.'

Even better! This can't be happening.

I'm beaming, of course. But the 'radical change' bit is a little unnerving. I've got plenty of ideas, yes, but I'm not sure if I'm really the radical type.

'Don't see this as a magazine for you any more. This is going to be more a magazine for your girlfriend.'

'It's going to be a magazine for women?'

'Correct.'

'O-kaay.'

I really try to process all of this. Really really try.

I know about women's magazines. I don't read them, obviously, they're for women but I know all about them. Yes, women's magazines: horoscopes and fashion tips and problem pages and real-life stories about falling in love with the guy who burgled your house and pictures of blokes with their tops off and MAKE-UP! Lots and lots of make-up.

I know about women's magazine editors too. They're all women! Glamorous, fashion-obsessed women. I'm a bloke. A gangly, some would unkindly say 'lanky', six foot four and a half (the half is important) tall bloke. I am not glamorous (if the clothes I'm wearing in any way suit me, which is unlikely, it's because my girlfriend Gaby has persuaded me not to buy it in the grey). A bloke. Editing a women's magazine. For women! What the hell are they playing at?

'Mark!'

'Uh-huh?'

'Are you listening?'

'Yes! Of course!'

'We need sales over 100,000 every week by the end of June or we'll close it. I'm not going to lie to you. Think about it tonight and Louise will speak to you tomorrow. You'll be reporting to her from now on if you decide to do this.'

And we hadn't even ordered our food yet.

Taken at face value, of course, this is exactly what I've been waiting for. Dreaming of. *Dying* for. The chance to run things. I love magazines, love everything about them. Love the way they grab you with an enticing front page. Love the way that reading one makes you feel like you're part of a special club that no one else is part of. I am obsessed.

But my passion for the job might not be enough. Can *Heat* be saved or is this just a great big poisoned chalice? Am I the one who'll go down with the ship, the editor who steered a multi-million-pound launch into the abyss?

Oh well, not a bad day all in all. There's still the thorny issue of me not being a woman but at least I didn't get fired.

Well, not yet anyway.

Thursday 9 December

Got up extra early this morning – 7.15 – and started making notes, bowl of Special K in one hand, pen in the other. I'm a morning person, which is lucky because I've got a meeting that I need to do lots of preparation for.

I pace around the flat. I live in Primrose Hill, an area becoming increasingly trendy with more and more celebrities coming to live here all the time.

Jude Law and Sadie Frost live two streets away with their kids in a huge house on a grotty street with uneven pavements and litter blowing everywhere.

Kate Moss lives five minutes away. She's always going round to Sadie 'n' Jude's and I often see them in the local minimarket, Shepherd's, picking junk food off the shelves and talking really loudly between themselves, too loudly, almost as if they need to get noticed all the time.

Just round the corner is Supernova Heights, Noel Gallagher's home for years. He's just sold it to Davinia Taylor, best friend of Kate 'n' Sadie, ex-girlfriend of Ryan Giggs and daughter of a multi-millionaire paper-mill owner.

Two minutes away is Liam and Patsy's old place. The graffiti's still there, and you'll often see Japanese girls posing and taking photos of each other outside.

Then, just ten minutes up the road, lives Ewan McGregor, one of the biggest movie stars of his generation.

I LOVE it.

I've lived here for a year with Gaby. I met her at work – she was the pretty girl in the next office. These days she works in interior design but sadly she can't do much with our place. We're in a rented flat with bare walls that are caked with dust. We don't hoover and the place is a mess. The least glamorous flat in London's most glamorous area.

Downstairs lives one of my heroes, an American record producer called Stephen Hague, who's probably best known for producing 'West End Girls' for the Pet Shop Boys. He came up and introduced himself on our first day in the flat.

'Hi, I'm Stephen from downstairs …'

'Oh my God, you're Stephen Hague!'

'Yeah. Listen, there appears to be water pouring through our ceiling.'

You know the hole on the side of a bath that lets water out if it goes over a certain level? Well, ours didn't have one. It's a disgrace! You'd expect Primrose Hill baths to come with their own entourage, each one scooping out excess amounts of water. Ours didn't even have an overflow.

(They say you should never meet your heroes. Is this kind of thing the reason why?)

Anyway, I made notes for an hour at home then for another 15 minutes on a packed tube into work just off Oxford Street. Trying to concentrate isn't easy when someone's paper is rubbing up against your face and someone else is standing on your foot. Also I can't help thinking back to the one previous time I met Louise Matthews and what an utter disaster it was.

Back in 1995 when the once-great *Smash Hits* was, to use one of its own phrases, going down the dumper, I was dragged in front of the board of Emap, the company I've worked for since I was 20 years old.

Smash Hits was embarking on yet another reinvention and I was the poor sod leading it. And there I was, in my nicely ironed shirt, just 24, achingly shy and telling the board of this huge publishing company that even though it was a pop music magazine, movie stars were the future of *Smash Hits*.

It was a stupid idea, of course, but the men in the room just wanted me to do SOMETHING and all of them murmured in positive tones. Louise Matthews was the only woman in the room that day and she didn't do any murmuring at all. In fact – if I remember correctly – she chewed gum and gave me a look throughout the presentation that basically said 'you're an idiot'. I probably was.

Hopefully, I thought, today she'll be a little nicer. Or at least a little more restrained.

In a small room at the back of the editorial office (two chairs, no table), Louise told me the plan: I am going to disappear for a few weeks into a small redesign room on a different floor to the *Heat* office with Lottie, our Art Editor. We are to completely reinvent the magazine. Ian Birch, the man whose job it is to oversee all the women's magazines in the company, is going to work with us to make sure we stay on track. Then Ian, Louise and I will come up with a strategy to save the magazine. And then Louise reiterated the closure plan ...

'Remember, if we don't get to 100,000 every week we are dead.'

'Do you know what, Sue said something like that to me yesterday.' She laughed.

'You're getting the message?'

'Kind of.'

It's clear that what everyone says about Louise is true – she doesn't mess about. Less scary than Sue, Louise gets her way by gentle persuasion, encouragement and infectious enthusiasm.

We started throwing around ideas and at last I had a chance to have my say: about how excited I was to finally be in charge, that I'd been spending my evenings manically typing up ideas for how the magazine could look … everything. She seems to approve of the way I'm thinking about it all. Thank God. Whatever she thinks, the truth is I've either got six months to make this work, or me and the entire *Heat* team will be picking up our P45s.

Tuesday 4 January 2000

Met with Ian Birch today in the foyer of the Berners Hotel round the corner from the office. Originally from Northern Ireland – with lilting accent still intact – Birchy is a tough, demanding guy who has edited some of the biggest and best magazines in the world. He has high standards.

I showed him my vision for the new-look *Heat* in written form. I want *Heat* to be a different kind of magazine, purposely the opposite of all the dull, fawning mags with cheesy stars that are already out there. This can be different.

This magazine was not a music magazine, not a TV magazine, not a film magazine, not a combination of the three. It was to be about celebs, the breed of people who could be famous for being in any of those three worlds or maybe even none of them. They were just famous. You'd recognise them if you saw them on the bus but often you wouldn't be able to quite place them.

To make it absolutely clear, for myself as much as Ian, I wrote our vision up in point form – it is to become the new magazine's manifesto:

* We're going to be the cool celebrity magazine for women.
* We'll be really funny.
* We'll have lots of exclusive interviews – and ask the questions people really want to see asked.
* We won't take celebrities that seriously.
* We'll take risks.
* No one can be boring in our magazine.

And then I showed him the latest issue, the one I and the team had finished putting together last week.

'But this is none of those things!' says Birchy, hardly able to keep his face straight.

He's right – the latest issue is drab and sooo boring.

Johnny Vaughan is on the cover, pulling his jacket collar up over his chin and grimacing.

Over the page are some tedious industry stories about people you've never heard of.

A few pages later a techy article about the latest bit of kit from Japan.

Then Johnny bloody Vaughan going on about himself over three pages.

And finally, 40 pages – 40 pages! – of TV listings with hardly any pictures.

It's obvious we have a mountain to climb.

It was a good session today, but I am convinced Ian doesn't think I can do this.

But then why would he? I'm not sure I can do it myself! I didn't tell him that, of course, but the fact is none of us have much confidence that we can pull this off. On the other hand, this is the sort of challenge I've been waiting for for years. I've been whinging all this time to Gaby at home that I want to actually be in charge and now I am, so I can't argue. I'll give it my very best shot. That's all anyone can ask. And anyway, I've got to stay positive.

Monday 21 February

After a frustrating month of research and team-rearranging we've finally started revamping the mag. We're in a small room just off someone else's office. Formerly a store cupboard, our den is about six feet by ten, has no windows and is unbelievably hot, even in February. And this is our home for the next six weeks. Ian pops in on the first day. He tells me, not that I didn't know, that I'm going to need a lot of help with the fashion and beauty content. Luckily he's found someone who can: Julian Linley, the brilliant and instinctive Deputy Editor at *More* magazine who's clearly destined for big things. I dare say they're putting him in with me for when I mess up. Maybe it should bother me that someone else is being given such a huge section of *my* magazine but the truth is it's a relief because I've got so much on my plate. In fact, I'm pathetically grateful.

Tuesday 22 February

Although I'm in my little store cupboard cooking up ideas, I'm still overseeing the magazine office. And we've got another problem. Because we're the most famous flop in the history of British magazines, no one will give us an interview. No one we want anyway. Because of this we've resigned ourselves to buying in interviews from other magazines and agencies. There's not many good ones about but this week, at least, we're running a juicy one: Noel Gallagher. I bloody love the Gallagher brothers. Until Oasis came along every guitar band was the same: too cool for their own good, monosyllabic in interviews and really really boring. It's a badge of honour to be moronic when you're in an indie band, it seems. No use AT ALL when you're running a magazine like ours. Oasis have changed all that – they bitch, they argue, they shout their mouths off and, in 'our' interview, Noel does this more than ever before.

The interview particularly dwells on the brothers' relationship with Robbie Williams. When Robbie left Take That three years ago he latched on to Oasis. Although he was in a cheesy boy band Robbie really wanted to be in an indie band. Oasis, more specifically. Within days of leaving Take That he drove his car, loaded down with champagne, on to the Glastonbury site and spent the next three days partying with his heroes. Soon after, the friendship cooled off, but the two parties have never discussed why. Until this piece.

'I've never been his friend!' says Noel, clearly riled. 'He was Liam's friend. Liam used to invite him to the gigs and stuff like that. I've been in dressing rooms with him but I wouldn't even consider him to be a friend of mine.'

The journalist, really onto something now, asks why.

'Why? Because he was in Take That! He's a fat dancer from Take That. Somebody who danced for a living! Stick to what you're good at, that's what I always say.'

Half with the new mag in mind, I've run that quote as the headline. It looks great on the page, a real result.

Wednesday 23 February

Our bought-in interview is being talked about everywhere. It's had a real impact. Robbie's not happy. He sent a wreath of white roses and lilies with a card to the showbiz desk at the *Sun*. The card read: 'To Noel Gallagher, RIP. Heard your latest album, with deepest sympathy. Robbie Williams.'

What a bitch! I love it when celebrities do stuff like this.

Monday 28 February

Jesus, now Liam's getting involved. This morning *The Big Breakfast* ran an interview where he says he'd break Williams' nose if he bumped into him. What have we started?

Friday 3 March

Most of the office is hungover this morning. It was the Brit Awards last night, the usual parade of show-offs, nearly there dresses (Liz Hurley, you've caused this) and stunts. I love the Brits; it's so ridiculous. And this year, a feud we created dominated the whole night. Robbie Williams came onstage and challenged Liam to a fight! 'So, anybody like to see me fight Liam?' he shouted to huge applause and cheering. 'Would you pay to come and see it? Liam, a hundred grand of your money and a hundred grand of my money. We'll get in a ring and we'll have a fight and you can all watch it on TV.'

Of course, everyone lapped it up. And the by-product of it all is that everyone's been running stories about our interview as a result.

This is incredible stuff. A magazine no one talks about suddenly getting acres of press. It's unnerving though – you get used to no one talking about your magazine so when they do you feel like you're put up there to be shot at. That's the only downside, though, because this sort of thing is great for business.

Friday 31 March

Gradually we're getting somewhere. With the fashion and beauty coverage being originated elsewhere I've been concentrating on the stuff I *can* do. Lottie's design is exceptional – fresh, uncluttered and very different to anything else on the market. Day-by-day, page-by-page we've been inventing the new-look *Heat*:

✱ Pacey, colourful interviews with headlines that shout out at you.
✱ Sets of photos with arrows that point stuff out and sarcastic captions that deride the very people we're celebrating.

✱ Pages and pages of designer shoes and bags with information on how to get hold of high-street copies for a fraction of the price – the idea is that the reader can look as good as the celebrities, but without spending all that money.

It's loud, anarchic and completely different to all the boring kiss-arse celebrity magazines already out there. I'm starting to feel really good about it. But there's still loads to do.

Tuesday 11 April

Five weeks to go until our first new-look magazine comes on sale. We urgently need a cover star. One that will triple our sales. Yeah, right. I've been thinking hard about all the potential options. In our position we don't have many.

While we were desperately trying to be a cool music, film and TV magazine last year, there was one huge event in the celebrity world, one single event that made 'celebrity' a far bigger deal than it ever was before.

The wedding of David Beckham and Victoria Adams had everything: glamour, opulence (it was rumoured to have cost two million quid!), a real kitsch, over-the-top, quality (at one point in the reception, the bride and groom sat on thrones). Also, because the event was bought up exclusively by *OK* magazine, we could all share in the fun. This was the world of celebrity as we'd never seen it before: up close and with us as part of it. We saw them cut the cake, laugh with their friends, walk up the aisle. We even saw the exact moment they became man and wife. We also learnt – and became hooked by – Victoria's story. It was fairytale stuff: dumpy, awkward teenager reinvents herself, becomes a pop star and marries her Prince Charming. Victoria was Miss Average made good and we'd followed her story through the media every step of the way: cheering for her, being pleased for her and fascinated that she'd stayed so normal. I remember being so struck by all of this at the time: how complete her reinvention was, how fascinating it must be if you were the age she was when she started and weren't happy about how you looked. Victoria is the story of the day. She has to be on the cover of our big relaunch issue. She is exactly the sort of person our new *Heat* readers will want to read about.

Only one problem – and it's a biggie. I'll have to convince her fearsome publicist Caroline McAteer that Victoria really should be on the cover of a magazine that no one is buying and everyone thinks is an embarrassing disaster at a time when she has nothing to promote. For free. We haven't got any money!

I need to get her on the phone first – and today, despite three attempts, I can't even do that.

Thursday 13 April
Two more messages left with Caroline today, one email and a fax. Nothing.

Tuesday 18 April
Made the last couple of appointments to our new-look team today. We've got a great set of section heads:

There's Julian: brilliant on features and fashion. Every few months he assigns part of the office wall to be his 'New Season' wall, full of pictures torn out of fashion magazines of how he wants to dress over the next few months.

Lottie is in charge of the design: prim and proper on the outside, but after a couple of drinks she comes out of her shell a bit. Okay, a lot. Very serious about what she does; there's been a few tears in our little bunker but it's only because she cares so much (that and the fact there's no windows, it's unbearably hot and is, in fact, merely a cupboard).

Dom – a former teen-magazine editor bussed in to make things operate a little more smoothly. A fearless interviewer, he loves the jokes and piss-taking of office life.

And there's Boyd. How do you describe Boyd? Me and Dom rescued him from a dull desk job at the Press Association and he's eternally grateful. Our 'TV coordinator', he's discerning, a great people person and seems to be able to make friends with every TV star he meets.

Slowly, as we all gel, we're forming a solid team spirit. Music gets cranked up in the office, silly pictures get stuck on the wall (usually animals wearing clothing, mass-murderers, polar bears kissing or naked men). In an average visit the suits will screw their noses up at at least five things they see or hear. Good. They're lucky we don't lock the doors.

Wednesday 19 April
Still no response from Caroline McAteer. But I will not be beaten.

Tuesday 25 April
I've been bugging Caroline McAteer for two whole weeks now. When I call she either sounds busy and 'will call me back' or I just get deflected by her assistant. Emails don't get replies. It's the classic brush-off. I'm becoming annoying so have left her alone for the past couple of days. Then today – finally – she agrees to see me. Tomorrow. Oh shit.

Wednesday 26 April
They say that Hollywood has the hardest-to-please publicists in the world and they're mostly right. It's always tough dealing with the LA PRs – abrupt, paranoid and impossible to get hold of, my time spent speaking to them at previous magazines has always been miserable. I'd often have to stay late in the office, dial them up in LA and – if they deigned to speak to me – spend half an hour promising their rubbish, unknown clients a feature before being told, after 30 minutes of small talk, that no I *can't* have an interview with Jennifer Aniston.

UK-based PRs are different: tough but essentially friendly characters who genuinely seem to like working with journalists.

Barbara Charone was born in the US, once a music journalist and has spent years protecting Madonna while also being jocular, down-to-earth and great company.

Gary Farrow is an incredible operator – his clients (and in his time he's worked with everyone from Jonathan Ross to George Michael) are all well served by his no-bullshit approach and strong relationships with all the UK tabloids.

Then there's Caroline McAteer.

Small, Irish, hard as nails, Caroline McAteer doesn't see eye to eye with most journalists. Most of the time, I get on with her. I've never wanted a scrap (whereas loads of tabloid hacks want nothing but), and I've been nice to her and on occasion even made her laugh. But still, getting Victoria Beckham on to the cover, whichever way you look at it, is a tough thing to ask.

I traipsed up Tottenham Court Road this morning to her office above Dreams ('the bed superstore'), with a pile of A3 boards on which we'd mounted dummy spreads for our new-look mag: the Star Style spreads with pieces about Versace and Dolce & Gabbana, our immaculate new beauty pages, articles about celebrity hangouts and hotels around the world, the five new must-visit boutiques in London. Yes, that's right; I chose all the pages shopping addict Victoria Beckham would be most likely to warm to! But also these are the pages that showed Caroline the brave new world we were soon to be in. A world miles away from the blokey magazine we'd been producing before.

I was shown into a tiny office at the back of the building; five minutes later she joined me.

'This better be good, you've been bugging me enough about it.'

She was right, it'd better. I launched into my spiel using the boards as props. I hadn't written down a word of what I was going to say, but had been living and breathing these pages so deeply I could talk for England about all of them. Apart from the fashion pages, of course. Then I was bluffing. Boy, was I bluffing.

I finished my presentation sweating from talking too quickly about fashion labels I know nothing about and hadn't even *heard* of two hours ago (Julian gave me a crash-course in high-end fashion before I left the office). After name-dropping Marc Jacobs and Dolce & Gabbana and God-alone knows who else (did I pronounce all the names correctly? Nooo, of course not, but I said them quickly so I was fine) I slumped on to a chair, the boards dropped to the floor and I grabbed my glass of water and gulped it down.

'So,' I say struggling to get my breath back, 'whaddaya think?'

'Really good. Really cool. I love the product pages.'

I beam.

'Thank you.'

This is in the bag. Heh-heh. Slam dunk!

'So ...'

I inhale.

'... when can we do the interview?' I grin my chirpiest grin.

'She's not doing any interviews.'

I let out a weird, high-pitched sound. '*WHAT?*'

'She's got nothing to promote. In August she will, but not now.'

No use. I need her now. I can't think of anyone else who can get us above 100,000 copies. I start to get desperate.

'Just ten minutes on the phone! We don't even need a shoot!' I'm begging now. I look pathetic.

'Mark – sorry. It's just not the right time.'

She begins to stand up. Is the meeting over already?

'But you like the new look! She'll love the new look.'

'Stop asking me! We'll talk again in a few months. I'm sorry, Mark. The magazine does look great though.'

No time for pride now, I decide. Copies of that day's papers are on the table and I pick one up ...

'Okay, what about all these ridiculous stories in the tabloids? The stories you keep saying are lies? Surely,' my voice goes up a few octaves at this point, '... *surely* she needs to put the record straight about these, otherwise people will think they're all true!'

Silence.

Caroline curls her lip, looks up at me and ...

'Actually, she probably would do something like that.'

I hold out a clammy hand.

'Deal!'

She smiles.

'Okay, deal. I'll call you tomorrow.'

I retained my composure until I got into the shaky, poky little lift that took me back downstairs, then punched the air. This interview, if it's good, could help us get the sales we want. I ran all the way back to the office to tell Louise and Ian.

'My God!' said Ian, in his typically infectious excited way.

'Mark, that's *amazing*,' said Louise.

We've never interviewed *anyone* very famous before really and now we've got the most famous person in Britain all to ourselves. I better not blow this.

Thursday 11 May

I'm sitting with Caroline in the reception of a posh accountants' office in Manchester waiting for David and Victoria to emerge from a meeting. Oh, to be a fly on the wall in *that* room. Me being here is the last throw of the dice for the magazine I have put everything into for the last year and a half. So today needs to go well ...

After half an hour Posh pretend-staggers out of the meeting, earlier than either of us were expecting her to – they've clearly let her leave early cos she was getting bored.

'Thank God for that!' she says when she sees us.

'Enjoyed that, did you?'

'Yeah ...'

Her face is full of sarcasm as she looks over her shoulder as the men and women in suits wander out.

'... loved it!'

She's in off-duty mode and you can tell that by the way she acts (like a kid who's been let off double maths, which in a way she just has been) and the way she looks: leisurewear, no make-up and baseball cap (bad hair day, clearly).

I like Posh and not just because she might well be about to save my career. I like her because she's funny and smart and sussed and doesn't take any shit. She's an interviewer's dream. And today, luck-ily, she's on top form and for nearly an hour and a half happily puts the record straight about various nonsense stories that have appeared in the tabloids over the last few months. But, as I hoped it would, the interview then strays into all sorts of other juicy areas: who she hates on TV, bitchy comments about other celebs. It's fantastic stuff. The revelations just kept coming: how her doctor has told her she is under-weight and is worried about her and how she was once told that she'd never be able to conceive.

I feared she'd clam up when the conversation moved on to all the anorexia rumours – the opposite was true. With Caroline sitting silently at the back of the room, Victoria – slowly and cautiously – gave her side of the story to me.

'I did look bloody awful. There are pictures [from around the time of the anorexia rumours] that I looked at and cried.'

'How much do you weigh now?'

'Seven and a half stone.'

'And did your doctor say that was normal for your height?'

'No. I should be about eight and a half or nine stone [she's 5' 6"]. But you know, who is totally happy with their body?'

The interview ended only when David came back from Boots – brilliantly, Victoria had sent him to buy a couple of things for her. There's a weird tension between these two, you can see it straightaway.

Stuff she says seems to embarrass him constantly. He gets niggled by her just being her – as they stand together in front of me he bristles. He is very serious: seems to have a set way of doing things and doesn't have the casual, easy, frivolous attitude to life most footballers have. Whereas she is the opposite of that – naturally awkward, she deflects that by being girly and silly. She was like that today. She hated the accountants' meeting – moaning about it throughout our time together – and talking to us is her idea of light relief. Most famous people hate interviews; I think Victoria sees it as time for a gossip. An outlet. In fact she talked so much that the two of them were going to be late leaving for their next appointment. David headed off to the ground floor reception to wait. And wait. And wait!

He phoned her.

She didn't answer.

Eventually she, Caroline and I got in the lift and as we only had one floor to go we pressed the next button down. It actually only took us to the mezzanine level and we piled out only to see David Beckham looking up at us, with a look of total despair. He screwed his face up as if to say 'duh' and watched us eventually make our way to the ground floor.

Something just doesn't quite ring true about this so-called perfect romance: it all seems very unbalanced.

Her last motion before rushing through the door is to put her shades on. I stood in the foyer and watched them walk out to the car – it's all rather like something out of a film. A single paparazzi photographer steps forward to get a shot. She pulls the cap down even further. Office girls over the road stop and stare. And then they are gone.

I can't quite believe it all happened, can't believe how good a story she's given me either. I'm euphoric.

Friday 12 May

My last day in the office for a fortnight and I'm working late. It's just me and the cleaner. I've written up the interview, painstakingly divided it into two – first rule of magazines: why let something run in one issue when it could be a two-parter – then started work on the cover. The cover will be finished by Lottie and Ian Birch on Monday but I want to establish the cover wording this evening. Up until now, desperate for sales, we've squeezed four or five stories on to the average cover. On this one we let our star dominate. Apart from a small sell at the top of the cover about the Baftas this will be all about Posh ...

EXCLUSIVE!
'My doctor says I should be nine stone'
Posh Spice answers all the rumours

Then along the bottom of the cover we go into more detail about what the interview covers.

Posh on David ...
Posh on Brooklyn ...
Posh on her weight ...

It's all or nothing. We hope that the appetite for the couple who are coming to epitomise this new decadent, moneyed celebrity world can save the magazine. We haven't gone through the 100,000 barrier yet – in fact the sales are at pretty similar levels to the ones I inherited – and if we don't with this we're finished. I head off on holiday not knowing if I'll have a magazine to edit in a week's time. I look back over my shoulder as I leave the office.

I might never be back.

POSH! "My anniversary gift for David"

This week's hottest celebrity news

heat

HOT NEWS

Jennifer back from honeymoon

Harry Enfield lays into Chris Evans

"I would have had sex with Mel in front of everyone"

EXCLUSIVE!

Big Brother

A week ago Randy Andy was kicked out the house. Has he been unfaithful to Mel? What does he think of Nick? Find out inside…

ROBBIE & GERI'S holiday photo album

9 771465 626005

CHAPTER TWO

Big Brother – it'll never work
May – September 2000

Friday 19 May

Aah, a relaxing holiday in the Greek Islands. Well, that's the idea.

This place is perfect: a small villa down a dirt track in the middle of nowhere. Just Gaby and me. And a pile of newspapers.

Being a magazine junkie I've managed to find a newsagent's somehow. I'm sad (I know this because Gaby keeps telling me I am – she can't abide the tabloids and certainly can't understand why anyone would want to read one when you're in a different country). But today I'm glad I went: I proudly returned from the shop with a copy of yesterday's *Sun*. Emap has supplied them with quotes from my interview and they've gone big on it. And in return, there, at the bottom of the article, is the reason we give them the stuff: a two-inch high thumbnail cover of *Heat*. Sharon Ring – an ex-editor of *OK*, now editor of a doomed Emap travel magazine called *Escape Routes* – has loads of contacts in the tabloid world so she's been calling them, gauging their interest in our exclusive before making sure (and this bit is vital) that the all-important cover picture appears on any coverage. That's what it's all about. Without the cover everyone will think this is an interview Posh has done for the *Sun* and that would be a disaster – for her (Posh has had such a hard time from the tabloids recently that she wants nothing to do with them) and for us. But it's there, it's huge (well, two inches high) and there's no doubt that this is a plug for our magazine.

I obsess about the article all afternoon. I'd set myself a target of 50 lengths in the villa's outdoor pool today and ended up doing nearly 80: I'm working out in my mind what this means for us. If 1 per cent of the people reading the *Sun* then decide to buy the magazine, that's 40,000 extra sales. Which would take us from our usual 80,000 to 120,000. Then there's part two of the interview, which should keep us over 100,000. But we won't know anything until I get back. I'm meant to be relaxing – it's my first holiday in nearly a year after all – but the stress of not knowing is starting to get to me a bit.

Monday 22 May

Happy Birthday to me! A landmark event, my 30th birthday, but the weather was not up to much, so today we just walked along the beach dodging the intermittent rain showers. I'm getting increasingly anxious about this week's issue, can't talk about anything else. Think Gaby wants to dump me.

Monday 29 May

Is a holiday actually a holiday if you end it more stressed than when you started it? A week ago I was a mildly concerned editor of a magazine; now, on the flight home, I'm a paranoid, anxiety-ridden fool who fiddles with strips of paper until they're in bits and just keeps shaking his head all the time. Fine in the privacy of my own flat but on a packed plane home I look deranged. The kind of person who you'd want to be sat well away from. Back in work tomorrow: D-Day.

Tuesday 30 May

Back in the office and I can't find a single soul who'll tell me if they know any sales information. What if it's a disaster and they're locked in a meeting deciding how and when to fold the magazine? It's early afternoon before the boss comes in – I'm sitting at my desk and look up as Louise walks through the door. 'It's 170,000. We might just have a hit on our hands.'

I freeze.

I can't quite believe this!

This isn't happening.

Louise is so matter of fact – with good news and bad – that sometimes you can't quite take it in. She also has utter confidence in everything she does. I, however, as I've shown to my possibly soon-to-be-ex-girlfriend, think most decisions I make are wrong. In this case, the pessimism makes the news twice as exciting. One by one people stop working, nudge each other and look over. Without thinking I get everyone together. It's not like they don't know anything's going on. I say a few words: telling the section heads, designers, subs and picture researchers who've stuck with me all this time how proud I am about what we've achieved with this issue but telling them (as I have to) that it's only one week's sale and there's a long way to go yet.

There are smiles where, for as long as I can remember, there have mainly been frowns. Someone buys half a dozen bottles of champagne. Executives I've never met before come in and slap me on the back. 'I always knew it could be done,' says one of them. Well, I'm glad you did!

Rushed home to tell Gaby the news. It's as much a relief for her as it is for me – we've had to deal with all sorts of worrying scenarios: that I'd have to go freelance and we'd have to cut our spending. That I'd be sacked and be out of work. What a relief.

Wednesday 31 May

I'm a born worrier and today – with a feeling of genuine euphoria around the office – is clearly not the day to remind people there's a long way to go. In fact, when I try it gets a bad reaction. So I shut myself into a meeting room and make notes, ideas about what we do next. The challenge we've been set is simple – sales have to be over 100,000 every week. Now we've done Posh, what on earth are we going to do next?

Monday 5 June

We're putting a real emphasis on news at the moment. News meetings are a really important part of our week now and the Monday morning one is vital.

We keep the numbers down but everyone plays their part.

News Editor Mat came from indie-music land – the *NME*. Passionate, eager to please and with great contacts. A truly lovely man.

We've just recruited Dan Wakeford from the *Sun* and he's fantastic, young and keen to impress. This is only his third week in the job but already he's doing well. While I was on holiday he shoved a copy of *Heat* into Tom Cruise's hands while he was walking along the street and got a snapper to take a shot – it really does look like Tom's carrying the magazine. And that was only Dan's fourth day in the office! He's a great talent.

Then there's Clara, our Picture Editor. I first met Clara when she sold pictures for an agency and would come from office to office selling her wares. Fiery, a tough negotiator and hard work, frankly –

needs reining in at times, but you'd rather have her on your side than on theirs.

Our Chief Sub is Julie – she makes sure we keep to our deadlines. Slightly older than most of the team but younger than all of us in spirit. A party girl, she can drink anyone under the table. Energetic and very popular – her background in high-frequency titles is essential.

Buzzing about our Beckham sale the meeting is dominated by what we can get on her next.

'We need more Posh stuff, something every week,' I say.

'Every week?' Mat raises his eyes to the ceiling but I know he's up for the challenge.

Dan has news. 'We'll get the first shots of her new look for the single in a few weeks, I spoke to Caroline yesterday.'

Ah, Caroline.

'Dan, let's keep her happy. Give her what she wants.'

'Okay, what else?'

Clara shows me some pictures.

'Julia Roberts throwing her shoes at Brad Pitt.'

'I'm sorry?'

She's winding me up.

'Okay, they're making a film! Still good, let's do a spread on these. Mat, what else?'

'This new TV show, a cartoon. There's a storyline where Britney's trying to pull Prince William.'

There's a real energy in these meetings now. We have a laugh too – very important for the morale and the atmosphere in the office. This isn't rocket science. But it feels right, and it's productive. Let's hope it continues.

More sales came in today. Our two Posh covers both sold well over 100,000. But based on very early figures, the one after, with a cobbled piece about Madonna on the front, sold bang on 100,000. We can't fall below that figure. Our closure threat is still there – if we don't deliver every week we're still in trouble.

Today we were offered a Robbie interview by a journalist who'd been commissioned by an Australian magazine. Only one problem: she's not sure if she's meant to be selling it on as she can't remember what kind of contract she signed. Robbie is such a big deal now that his management company usually want to have a say in where his interviews run – in Britain, where he couldn't be any *more* famous, they don't want him appearing anywhere. They think he's over-exposed and people will get fed up of him, so no one in the UK gets interviews. But in Australia – where he isn't as famous – the management and record company need him everywhere.

However, this journalist needs the money and she's prepared to sell it to us for a fee. And we're desperate. This 100,000 thing is addictive – all I can see in my mind is next week's cover and the words:

ROBBIE – EXCLUSIVE INTERVIEW

We need this. We're probably not supposed to do it, but I don't feel I've got much of an alternative.

I email her and tell her she has her deal, but decide not to tell anyone else how this came about. The thought of such a big interview is huge, it's exciting, but the guilt is pretty sizeable too – if the contract does preclude her selling it on we could get into trouble and she could too. But we have nothing else because no one will give us a damn thing.

Thursday 8 June
Thursday is *Heat*'s press day and the biggest day of the week. The main job of the day is getting the cover done. Essentially, it's me, Lottie, and my bosses Louise and Ian peering at a screen. Other members of the team walk past from time to time to pass comment, slag off the cover star's outfit or, occasionally, say 'who's that?' (always slightly worrying, that last one).

The Robbie cover looks really exciting and leads off with a quote about Nicole Appleton who was engaged to Robbie a couple of years before and is now going out with his mortal enemy – Liam Gallagher. It's incredible stuff ... that he was never in love with Nicole, how he's often tempted to take drugs, how much he misses Take That. Reading it, I conclude that Robbie fancies the journalist, because he's flirting with her throughout and telling her everything – either that or he's just so relaxed in the knowledge that no one will ever read it outside of Australia that he feels he can say anything he wants. If he does think that, he's being very naive, as some fan site is bound to put it on the web in a matter of weeks. We're selling it in a suitably hard fashion:

SENSATIONAL INTERVIEW
Robbie!
'I've never been in love. Engaged? Yeah, but ...
that doesn't really mean anything does it?'

As with the Posh piece I've divided the interview into two and sent it off to the printers with a mouth-watering plug at the end – Robbie will talk openly about how he wants to become a dad and (most enticing of all) he'll tell *Heat*'s 100,000 (or so) readers which pop star he secretly fancies. This is dynamite. They'll be gagging for part two!

Tuesday 13 June

This afternoon we got a legal letter from Robbie's lawyers. They say we haven't the right to print the interview and are suing us. Oh shit. I've had a couple of legal letters before but this is scary and there's no room for compromise. Tonight I have just one thought on my mind:

'We're being sued. We're being sued.'

As an editor you never get used to the idea of being sued. It's rotten – the first time it happens and the hundredth. The feeling of doom when your PA walks over and puts three or four pages of A4 face down on your desk. All my PAs throughout the years have given me the same look as they do it: that mixture of sympathy and 'boy, are *you* in the shit now'. You know it's a legal letter from their look. You can also make out through the paper that densely typed text, with the official bit in bold type at the top of the letter and the bits in inverted commas where they quote the words from your article that seemed so smart and funny when you wrote it but now seem reckless and ridiculous. 'Great,' you think, 'this is going to cost my bosses, the very ones I'm supposed to be impressing, a HUGE amount of money.' Lawyers' letters are one of the few things that can get a good editor fired: it shows a lack of judgement, embarrasses the whole company and can cost a fortune they hadn't budgeted for (lots of companies do have budgets for legal costs but they always assume it won't be spent and it can go on something nicer instead).

The more a magazine pushes the boundaries – and, after all, two parts of the *Heat* philosophy are 'we won't take celebrities that seriously' and 'we'll take risks' – the more this sort of thing will happen.

I went home tonight feeling truly sick. I know that this won't be the only time a celebrity will come after us. Better get used to it.

The really sickening thing about today? Robbie's lawyers won't let me run my beloved part two.

Wednesday 14 June

Our main mission for today is to try and overturn Robbie's ban on part two of 'our' interview.

I'm trying everything. At the other end of the phone, our lawyer Richard bats away every pathetic attempt I make.

'Just say to them there's no point in stopping part two because the worst bits have already run in part one.'

'But they say you shouldn't have run any of it.'

'Hmm. How about we only run some of it.'

'They won't go for that.'

'I know, offer Robbie some money for his charity, then they'll let us print it.'

He's really not sure but agrees to give it a go.

Two hours later he calls back.

'Robbie wants to thank you for the money ...'

Yes!

'... He says the charity will be very grateful ...'

I am a genius!

'... But you still can't run it.'

Oh great. Our next cover: gone. Also, and this hurts, the 100,000 readers we've managed to get to read the magazine are now going to feel let down by us because we can't provide them with something we promised.

A thoroughly depressing day – and still no cover for the next issue.

Thursday 15 June

Press day. Everything has to leave the office by the end of today – if it doesn't we risk not having the magazine on sale next Tuesday. The team arrived at work this morning to see me there pacing around the office like some demented zoo animal. I've had an idea – just cos we're not allowed to put part two of the interview on the cover doesn't mean we can't put Robbie on there. So we have done! With Kylie, the pop star he was about to reveal he fancied.

Everyone piles in to the cuttings cupboard – filing cabinets full of articles and interviews and news stories all cut out (badly) from newspapers. Mat Smith, our brilliant News Editor who deserves far more challenging assignments than this one, finds a quote from Robbie saying how much he likes Kylie: 'She's gorgeous and frail, I feel like I want to protect her and keep her under my wing.'

Our junior news guy Paul Croughton – several hours later – finds one from Kylie about Robbie. 'I think he's well fanciable,' the quote goes. 'It might happen. He's very cute.'

Put them together and ... BINGO! The same story as the one we're not allowed to run!

Today, we've had a real 'Eureka!' moment. Since the Posh interview – and the increased pressures on me to maintain that 100,000+ sale – I've been constantly frustrated by the brick wall we're up against. No one big gives us interviews, no one big (in Robbie's case) even wants us to have second-hand interviews. Yet the tabloids (who don't get them either) sell millions a day by being clever, cheeky even. It's that attitude that *Heat* needs. Why wait around for scraps when we can get in there, roll up our sleeves and get what we want, what our readers what. A tabloid, but in magazine form. It's more expensive than a paper, sure, but the pictures are in glossy colour, the ink doesn't come off in your hands and you're not ashamed to read it on the train.

Today, we delivered the kind of magazine we wanted by being clever and cheeky and without having to butter up famous people and the team of people around them. I can't face doing that every single week. It is soul-destroying and rarely works anyway. Getting an interview with a million-selling singer or top Hollywood star, week in week out, would involve doing all of the following:

1. Suck up to a PR. This could take several months.
2. Promise the PR the world – copy-approved interviews, retouched photos, the lot.
3. Arrive at the interview, discover that famous person will only discuss how great it was to work with their latest co-star, and not their boyfriend/girlfriend, person they're having an affair with, their famous friends, money, houses, the drugs they take or the partying (i.e. anything interesting).
4. Eventually manage to persuade the star to give you a bit of 'colour'

– some piece of gossip that they think is amazingly revelatory but is actually the same anecdote they trot out in every interview.

5. Get it all approved, put the words together with the retouched pictures (where the celeb no longer looks like them or even human) and then put the magazine on sale.

That is what incredibly famous people (and their agents and publicists) will put magazine editors through every day of the week if they're allowed to.

But readers are now getting bored with all that, they realise that they're not getting to see the real person and they're aware that, essentially, this is someone selling product with the least possible bit of effort on their part. Sales of glossy mags are falling because people want something a bit real. Tabloid papers have done it for years but now there's an appetite among magazine readers for this too.

Quotes given when celebs are not on their guard or don't have PRs breathing down their necks is what we want.

This way we can deliver the stories people really want even if we don't get an interview. Readers want their magazines fast, pacey and unapproved now – they don't want retouched photos and bland copy-approved interviews any more. They don't believe them.

I think the tables may have turned. Maybe now we can call the shots.

Wednesday 28 June
Another great day. The marketing team burst into a news meeting with some fantastic news – both Robbie issues (the one with him on his own and the one with him and Kylie) sold over 100,000. We still stand a chance of survival – the average sale from mid-May to now is just over 100,000. The team are working long hours, fuelled by adrenalin and the occasional glass of management champagne (they LOVE us now!)

Friday 14 July
Today ten people have gone into something called the Big Brother house. I've been hearing about the Dutch version of this show for several months now and I have to be honest: the whole thing unnerves me. Foreign TV has always been more out there than ours – Chris Tarrant has got several series out of what mad Japanese people put

themselves through for fame – but this seems to be taking an odder, darker turn. The stuff I hear about the show makes it sound wilfully cruel: people are locked in a house for nine weeks, they don't know what time of day it is, they're woken up in the middle of the night by some shadowy figure called Big Brother. Weird. Its arrival on Dutch TV was met with criticism from a media concerned about the effect on the contestants. I'm not sure either. Plus, the hype is unbearable. We've run a few bits on the UK version of the show but I'm sceptical. 'Let's not go overboard on this,' I told the TV team yesterday, leading from the front as always. 'Just because the rest of Europe's gone mad for it doesn't mean Britain will. This could well be a huge flop.'

Tuesday 18 July

The first episode of *Big Brother* – covering the first few days that the contestants have been in the house – went out on Channel 4 this evening. The show began with the housemates wheeling their suit-cases along a path into this characterless box. So far, so dull. But within minutes they were arguing, engaging in power struggles and taking their clothes off. I realised halfway through that I know nothing and it will be huge. In fact it's amazing. There's nothing like watching how people interact, flirt, get annoyed and cope under pressure. It's a little unsettling too: voyeuristic with a real sense that you're seeing something you shouldn't.

Wednesday 19 July

Boyd came over with the news that 3.7 million people watched last night's show – huge for Channel 4. I look like an idiot in the office. Might have to reverse my opinion about covering it in the mag.

Friday 28 July

In Edinburgh for the weekend with Gaby but it hasn't gone to plan. The plane was delayed and my plans to watch the first *Big Brother* 'evic-tion' show have been wrecked (yep, I'm now addicted). Our taxi pulled up at the hotel about 20 minutes before the end of the show, we checked in and dashed up to the room just in time to see sloaney Sada evicted. The scenes are incredible – scary even. Davina McCall is stand-ing in front of a baying crowd – some of whom have placards for God's sake! – as some poor woman prepares to come up out of a TV house she's been locked in for two weeks. This is proper edgy TV, the sort of thing that scares you. The power of the show has hit me tonight. It's extreme but exciting and absolutely fascinating: what if someone in that crowd starts throwing things? Could someone rush the barriers and grab hold of a contestant they don't like? I can't stop thinking about it.

Thursday 3 August
Tonight, two of the contestants on *Big Brother* have snogged. Brilliant! Now we've got a TV programme! Andy (bit big for his boots) and Mel (far more streetwise, if a little self-conscious) kissed at just after 9 p.m. this evening. He's clearly into her; she's not that into him. 'You shouldn't have done that,' she said while grinning, 'you couldn't handle me in the real world.'

Andy, clearly not ready to retreat, replied with a rather smug, 'I'm willing to give it a try.'

Then they got interrupted. Booooo!

Friday 4 August
The snog. The snog! The office can talk about nothing but the snog. They're obsessed. In the middle of the office Clara and her picture team are in full swing …

'She's just playing with him! He's putty in her hands.'

'Rubbish, she's just playing it cool because the cameras are on her.'

'We'll see – it won't last two minutes outside, betcha.'

I know why they're so gripped as well – for all the great dramas or incredible fly-on-the-wall documentaries, TV has never seen this realness. We've never been there when someone falls for someone or even just decide they fancy them. And now we are. It's like the *OK* cover of the Beckham wedding: what people loved about that magazine was that they, the reader, could be there when the two of them became man and wife. But this TV show is even better, because now we can be there when people kiss for the first time. *Heat*, I have decided, should be the magazine that's there at the most important moments of a celebrity's life: when they fall in love (or lust), split up or are in despair. We can be the magazine equivalent of a reality TV show, a soap opera but about real people who just happen to be famous. I think I knew this all anyway, but *Big Brother* has crystallised everything for me. Suddenly everything seems so obviously clear.

If we're discussing it in the office chances are hundreds of thousands of other people are gossiping about 'Randy Andy' and Mel, too. Does she like him or was she just being kind? Was he forcing himself on her to try and avoid eviction, by suggesting to the people at home that something more would happen if they kept him in? If he did think that, it didn't work. Tonight he is the second *Big Brother* evictee. And Mel isn't that bothered. She already has her eye on shy Irish housemate Tom ...

Thursday 10 August

As is our Thursday tradition, the inner cabal is convened and we design the cover, But this week I'm having a minor panic. The semi-finished design has a photoshoot we did with Randy Andy on it – and I'm grabbing people from around the office to have a look. 'Okay,' I'd say pointing at it, 'but is he actually famous? I mean, I know he's on telly but he's not a celebrity is he?'

I've agonised over this. It seems the weirdest thing – I get that the show's huge but here's someone – an ordinary guy who's been locked in a house for a few weeks – who's not really a celebrity at all, but he's on our cover. Well, he is a celebrity, sort of. But he's not a film star, and he doesn't make records ... First rule of celebrity magazines: put a celebrity on the cover, stupid!

Julian, thinking instinctively as usual, reckons it's a great idea: 'Everyone's talking about him in the office – don't worry about it.'

Louise is freaked out by it – she just doesn't get *Big Brother* and thinks we're going 'too far, too soon'. Still, we've gone with it.

Tuesday 15 August

Spent the evening at the BBC. Because of the magazine's ever-increasing profile quite a few of us are getting asked to be on TV shows and I encourage anyone asked to say yes. It's essentially free advertising – and if we don't say yes to sitting on some TV sofa our rivals probably will.

Tonight I was asked to be on a show called *Liquid News* and I jumped at the chance. I love *Liquid News* and have been hoping for a while that I'd get asked to be on. A daily round-up of the latest entertainment news, the show is most notable for its presenter: a large, wry, some would say sarcy, gay, *Eurovision*-obsessed guy called Christopher

Price. The show looks like a normal news bulletin – guy in a suit sits behind a desk, cueing in reporter-fronted news items. But all the reports are about the world of celebrity and Price treats the ridiculous characters of that world with the disdain they require. It's a great show and I am flattered to be asked on it, even if it takes up much of my evening (it goes out live at 7 p.m.). In many ways it's a companion to what *Heat* does, the moving picture version of our funny, sarcy take on showbiz. Today's other guest was our current cover star Randy Andy and (ridiculously) I felt really star-struck. Of all the people you meet in this job why the *hell* am I star-struck about a guy who isn't famous and has just been filmed in a house doing bugger all for a few weeks? No idea. But I was. It's pathetic. Show went well and they asked me back on.

Wednesday 16 August
Interviewed Jamie Theakston this morning for our next cover. An ex-kids' TV presenter who's just recently gravitated to bigger things, he's being hounded by the tabloids at the moment – he wanted to be interviewed outside of central London because he's being followed by the paparazzi day and night, so we met at the Cobden Club, a grand, showy private members' bar – all drapes and secret alcoves – frequented by the ultra-cool West London brigade. You think the Groucho Club/Soho House lot are cool? The West London bunch look down on that crowd. Too many suits and expense accounts for the Notting Hill bunch, the clientele here are ten years younger and would rather die than wear trainers you can actually buy in Britain. They wear jeans that fall beneath your arse (on purpose), grow silly little beards and greet each other with complicated handshakes. It's like I've wandered into an alien world, Planet Stupidly Cool.

Theakston's nervous and cagey from the moment I shake hands with him – although that's not that surprising. The last few occasions he's been written about haven't gone well. One tabloid journo concluded he was an egomaniac ('for 20 minutes all Jamie did was talk about himself' the piece said – surely the point of interviews?), his relatively new relationship with a very famous, older woman (Joely Richardson) has been pulled apart and – worst of all – an ex-girlfriend apparently told a gossip columnist that he had a small penis! Whoops. This has led to all sorts of hassle for him: he's been joked about by his friend Sara Cox on the radio, opinion columnists have mocked him and, on one particularly memorable day, a lorry driver shouted 'pencil dick' at him as he walked down the street. With his mum!

I'm genuinely shocked. 'That actually happened?'

'Yep,' he says looking mortified, 'then I had to explain the whole thing to her because she doesn't read those newspapers.'

So no wonder he's so nervy – although he opens up a bit, he won't talk about exes, is overly formal and uptight about certain 'hot spots', so answers end up sounding over-rehearsed and naff (having a child would be 'a blessing' he 'reveals' at one point. 'I'm sure the birth of my first child will be a huge defining moment in my life').

Eventually, though, I do get him to open up when I ask about Joely because he is so loved up: how he had to miss a big Euro 2000 match because she'd hurt her leg, about the sacrifices he makes for her. He feels he can trust us and he's right. *Heat* is gradually getting to be known as the safe enclave of celebdom – battered and bruised by the tabloids? Come to *Heat* and we'll be nicer to you. I like that approach. It feels right for me. It doesn't come easily to me, being mean. Anyway, Theakston's a nice guy and he appreciates that we're giving him a fair hearing. In fact he's so relaxed that a shot we hoped he'd pose for but assumed he'd refuse to do – of him at a urinal, a reference to willy-gate – he's quite happy to do. Increasingly people like him like us – because we're the good guys.

Thursday 17 August
It's insane the effect a TV show can have on an office of people. Granted, it doesn't take much to put the *Heat* team off their work but today is extreme. After becoming aware of his manipulating ways the housemates confronted *Big Brother*'s bad guy Nick Bateman and, prompted by this, the show's producers chucked him out! We watched this unfold on the Internet – live footage is streamed 24/7 but the system keeps crashing so we only watch a few minutes at a time before it happens again and we have to reboot the computer. But gradually the entire office wandered over to the poor designer's computer, people from other parts of the building even dropping in. Somehow, this all feels like a big cultural event and we've all found ourselves stopping work to get our voyeuristic kicks from the pictures. I remember, at primary school, loads of us gathering around the big school telly to watch the shuttle take-off. Surely some bloke wheeling

a suitcase out of a house can't have the same must-see effect? But, weirdly, it does. This is the world of celebrity, 21st-century style.

I convened an emergency meeting in the hallway.

'So he's gone?' I ask Julian.

'Yeah, the press team just called.'

'He's going to have to go into hiding, isn't he? The whole nation hates him, don't they?'

Everyone shrugs. We've no idea if this guy – because of his actions on a TV show – has just gone and ruined his entire life. Yes it's just a TV programme, but right now *Big Brother* feels like the centre of our world. I've cleared six pages for the Nasty Nick departure story, and I've just called up the marketing department suggesting they print 50,000 extra copies next week.

Tuesday 22 August

The Randy Andy issue has been a huge seller for us – over 150,000. The Nasty Nick one will surpass that, I'm sure. The definition of celebrity has just widened.

Anyone is now a celebrity. We've been the first to realise this and it's something that is helping us immensely. No one else has picked up on it. The papers are dismissing it as a minority Channel 4 show and aren't covering it. The other magazines are run by people who are – frankly – too old and just don't get it (which is crazy, especially as these offices will be packed full of twenty-something junior writers and designers who will be talking about nothing else). *Big Brother* is where we can really make ourselves stand out from the competition. And, rather brilliantly, there's an endless supply of new faces for us to cover too. It could have been invented for us.

Monday 4 September

Next week is the final of *Big Brother* and we're compiling a special preview issue. We sat around thinking of ideas and, half-joking, I suggested starting a helpline for *Big Brother* obsessives who can't face life without it. I've become convinced it's a great idea: a German radio station did one when Take That split up and it's kind of the same. We've persuaded Phillip Hodson, the Agony Uncle on the eighties Saturday morning kids' TV show *Going Live*, to man a phoneline for five hours the day after the final and we'll plug it in the new issue.

Thursday 7 September

Put the issue to bed, with the phoneline number printed in huge 48-point type on a really prominent page. Other people aren't as keen as I am: in fact, it's become known as 'Mark's helpline' in the office as I'm the only one who thinks it's a good idea. Not so sure myself any more.

Friday 15 September

The *Big Brother* final! Buoyed by some great sales and fascinated by the programme, we are going to work late, probably until about 3 a.m., putting together an end-of-series souvenir issue – the first 30 pages is full of interviews, analysis and pictures of the best moments. Craig, the amiable scouser, won. The media went *Big Brother* crazy – our PRs received seven or eight requests for interviews with me! I only had time to do one – a TV interview for an American TV channel. When I got there they didn't seem interested in who I thought would win, my opinions on the final three or anything. They were just obsessed by my STUPID helpline idea. It really is not an idea that stands up that well to examination: 'Do you really think your readers will need counselling when a TV programme ends?' No, we did it as a joke. 'What are you trying to say about people who watch this TV programme?' Nothing, it was a joke. And so on. The papers have even been writing about it. We're going to look like idiots.

Saturday 16 September

Slept badly last night. I wasn't going to have a great night's sleep anyway as I didn't get home until 4 a.m. but I woke up at 10 a.m. just as the helpline opened. In the cold light of day it seems like such a dumb idea. I have visions of idiots phoning up lovely Phillip Hodson and being rude to him or just putting the phone down. The PR for the show rings to say that 10 million watched the final part of last night's show. And 7.7 million of them voted. Bloody hell!

Monday 18 September

How early can you call a counsellor? Do they sleep in? Get up early? I managed to hold out calling Phillip Hodson until, ooh, five past nine. Incredible news: 2,000 people called our helpline. As he was the only person manning the phone for the five hours the line was open, he could only answer just under 100 of them. But the response was astonishing – I was expecting prank-callers, piss-takers and the occasional media enquiry but what we got was real emotion. One girl phoned in in tears because she loved Craig, who won, but felt let down when she read a taboid interview that made him sound like a bit of a love-rat. One softly spoken woman told Phillip that Nasty Nick was haunting her dreams night after night and she didn't know what to do. Several said the series ending made them realise they didn't have enough friends and decided to try and meet more or join clubs and societies. Many rang in just to say they felt silly being upset about a TV show ending – you and me both!

This really has been an incredible success. Lots of people laughed when they knew we were doing it – *I* didn't even take it that seriously. But this show has somehow affected people's lives. It is truly involving TV – and I can't pretend I am any different from some of the people calling the helpline.

But it's now three days since the show ended and I'm missing it – nothing to watch on TV, hurriedly making plans to fill up spare evenings. I made the mistake of telling Julie this. What was I thinking – with a perma-glint in her eye she relishes any chance to take the piss: 'Is that helpline of yours still open? Maybe you should give it a ring?'

Cheers.

Tuesday 26 September
Now *Big Brother*'s over, Gaby and I have been able to get away for a bit. Nothing to watch on telly any more anyway so the Algarve – still boiling hot at this time of year – is the perfect place. It's certainly been a less-stressed holiday than the last one. We fly home tomorrow and I feel nicely refreshed. Even better, this morning I got my first work text of the trip – from Lottie, who won the battle to tell me the good news – the end-of-series *Big Brother* souvenir issue has sold over 200,000 copies, the first issue to do that many. I can die a happy man.

Wednesday 27 September
Woke up at 5.30 a.m. in a total panic. *Big Brother*. It's finished. What the hell are we going to fill our pages with now?

She's back! Zoë Ball talks sex, Norm & babies

This week's hottest celebrity news
£1.35   10 - 16 March 2001

heat

Issue 107

How *did* she do that?
Geri's amazing new look

New body, new hair, new friends

PICTURE EXCLUSIVE!

Inside Liam & Nicole's NEW dream home

PLUS **The Brits!** the winners, the dresses — and the scandal

CHAPTER THREE
Geri wants my children
October 2000 – September 2001

Wednesday 18 October

Thank God for the Spice Girls. Thank God for Caroline McAteer. I spent all day backstage at *Top Of The Pops*, smuggled in as part of the Spice Girls entourage. *Top Of The Pops* has a rule that only their own magazine's journalists are allowed in so I have signed in as a friend of the band. I'm here to write an access-all-areas piece and, God, it's exhausting.

Mel B's gorgeous daughter Phoenix Chi is running around from person to person asking for food. 'Have you got any chips?' she'd say. 'No, sorry Phoenix.' Then on to the next person: 'Have you got any chips?' When they say no she moves on to the next. Kids are *shameless*.

Posh spends all her time posing, preening, asking if she looks all right and popping back into their dressing room endlessly. Her mum's there too. 'Mum, how does this look?' 'You look fine.' 'Really?' 'Yes! Fine, gorgeous.' She then heads over to the mirror and shakes her head as she fiddles with her outfit then her hair.

Emma is lovely (Emma is always lovely – friendly, polite, an absolute dream).

Then there's Mel C.

Mel C isn't really speaking to me, which isn't ideal when you're supposed to be interviewing her. Since *Big Brother* ended we've gone Spice Girls crazy. Scared silly about our sales falling off now the show's over, we've been covering everything they do, no matter how tenuous: who's put on weight, who's lost weight, who's bought a new dress. We're a celebrity magazine after all: we can get away with this sort of stuff. Particularly of interest, though, has been Mel's love life. Earlier this year the (completely incorrect) tabloid story was that she was a lesbian – she was very close to her female assistant and the two holidayed together. Since the rumours died down she's gone man-mad: there was a fling with Robbie Williams, an affair with one of the boys in Five and now a new man, a guy called Dan who's in a band called Tomcat, who is here, skulking in the shadows. The team with the Spice Girls are doing everything they can to keep me away from him. No, you can't speak to him. No, you can't take photos. In fact, it becomes patently obvious that she doesn't really want me here at all.

'Ah, *Heat* magazine!' she says with a fake cheesy grin. 'I'm not talking to you.'

'Aww, come on Mel! Don't be like that! How's the new bloke?'

'Get lost.'

She grabs Dan's hand and wanders off.

I decide to follow them. It's my journalistic duty. Some would call it stalking but that's patently not true – after all, I'm with the band. For the next five minutes I wander down corridors, ducking out of the way when she looks over her shoulder.

Eventually I find them through a side door, snogging each other's faces off. Ten minutes later they're down a different corridor doing the same.

Okay, Mel. We get the idea. You're not a lesbian. Don't shove it down our throat (or his).

Once she's onstage I manage to escape Caroline's clutches for ten minutes and grab Dan. He's like a love-sick puppy, looking wistfully at Mel C as she throws shapes for the camera. 'She acts really hard when she's up there but she's not, you know. She's dead soft.'

Mel comes offstage and eyes me with huge suspicion. I know she saw me talking to him. She steers him away from me for the rest of the day.

Tuesday 31 October

Robbie and Liam are still at each other's throats. Tonight was the *Q* Awards at the Park Lane Hotel and they were both there. While most other music awards shows have got dull and corporate, the *Q* Awards is still an unruly, drunken bear pit. Drinks are thrown, people get into scraps and – because it's not televised – they say and do whatever they want. This is the off-duty awards and anything goes.

Sitting in the basement after the award ceremony had taken place there was a sudden commotion two tables away. Liam had been taunting Robbie all night and Robbie – surrounded by his own entourage and four security guards – didn't seem that bothered. Until, that is, Gallagher started chanting insults about Kylie. Then Robbie got more and more agitated.

Liam was drunk but that's no excuse for being purposely vile.

As she walked a few yards in front of him he shouted the immortal words, 'Get your tits out, you lesbian!'

I couldn't believe this was happening – there was Liam Gallagher screaming in Kylie's direction. Suddenly everyone around us felt incredibly uncomfortable. Robbie glares at him. But Liam isn't finished.

'Yeah ... and write your own songs.'

At this point, Robbie saw red. He walked over to Liam, fists clenched by his side. Then, just yards away, he unclenched his fists and did a swift about turn, just yards from Liam's table. Part of me was disappointed. Is that bad? Feuds sell magazines and fights make for good picture spreads.

Tuesday 14 November

Today Dominic Smith interviewed Kelly Brook. Kelly Brook isn't happy and really doesn't want to do the interview and I don't blame her. But she has to – she's in a play in London called *Eye Contact* and the contract she's signed says she has to do magazine interviews. Whereas some celebs hate magazines because of some perceived slight or because they didn't pump up their ego enough, Kelly Brook probably hates us because one week last autumn we paid a journalist to watch every minute of *The Big Breakfast* – the show she was presenting – and write down every mistake she made. Every fluff, every mispronounced name, everything. The article had a huge effect on her – it led to an endless stream of tabloid criticism, industry speculation and, eventually, she was removed from the show. We didn't make the decision to fire her – the show's producers did – but we are still partly responsible. How responsible she thinks we are we were about to find out ...

Dom was the right man for the job. A tough, persistent interviewer he loves challenges like this. Any other journalist would be nervous as they're heading out to do an interview this contentious, Dom just grabbed his tape recorder and off he went. I wait in the office for news and when I get some it seems Dom's charmed the pants off her. She has a bit of a rant (quite rightly) about what we did. 'It was a delicate situation,' she told Dom, 'I'd just started my first TV job and I didn't really need that.'

Dom – who opposed the original piece anyway – is sympathetic and gets real raw emotion out of her. She knows it was my idea so gives Dom an easy ride. If she ever bumps into me, I don't think I'll get off so lightly.

Saturday 18 November

Catherine Zeta-Jones and Micheal Douglas marry in New York. A photographer sneaks into the wedding posing as a waiter and sells the pictures to *Hello* magazine, in spite of the happy couple's exclusive deal with *OK* magazine. The shit's really going to hit the fan now.

Friday 22 December

Madonna married Guy Ritchie at a remote castle in Scotland today. It's just three days before Christmas but still the local village is packed with journalists and photographers, all standing outside the gates to the castle freezing and getting bugger all. One photographer, fed up with the cold and with his agency screaming down the phone at him, hides in a piano inside the chapel so he can get some exclusive pictures of the ceremony. Sadly he was discovered a few hours before the vows. It's a sign of how big the whole celebrity thing is now, that the wedding becomes such a circus.

Tuesday 2 January 2001

First day back and we've only got four days to do the issue. Today's news meeting is vitally important.

I'm trying to get the meeting started but Dan and Clara are distracted – they're poring over some photographs.

'You won't believe these.'

'Dan, try me ... Jesus!'

There, before my very eyes, is pop singer Billie (a mere 18) sitting on the knee of Chris Evans (34).

'Dan, tell me they're joking. This is a wind up.'

'Nope, he's just bought her a Ferrari. Delivered it to her just before Christmas.'

'Billie can't drive!'

'Correct.'

The consensus of the meeting – and the *Heat* office generally – can be summed up in one sentence: dirty old man.

This relationship isn't going anywhere.

Wednesday 24 January

The big TV show at the moment is ITV's *Popstars*. The show features a series of singers going through a prolonged audition to become part of a pop band. Star of the show at the moment is a Glaswegian student called Darius. Darius is an over-the-top show-off whose animated cover versions have become cult viewing. ITV have tipped us off that he's getting the boot in Saturday's show (the series is pre-recorded) so today we interviewed him. He is now far more modest but still thinks he's going to have a number one record. We're putting him straight on the cover next Tuesday.

Saturday 27 January

So glad we've got Darius for Tuesday's cover. ITV said his final show was going to be good and they weren't wrong. His performance of Britney Spears' '...Baby One More Time' is preposterous: full of exaggerated gestures and odd quirks. He is a true *Heat* character: funny, memorable and everyone's talking about him. No one has picked up on him other than us – the competition has been left well behind.

Thursday 15 February

Another great day: at midday we announced our latest sales figures for the six months between July and December last year. Our average sale was 172,311 copies! The *Guardian* have asked me to write a piece about how well we've done – it's a great opportunity to show off. 'We've got a brilliant, loyal team working hard every single day,' I wrote. 'The management have been nothing short of inspirational' (what a creep!) before building up to the truly self-satisfied, 'There's no bigger thrill than seeing people reading *Heat* on buses, raving about it to their friends, talking about it on the radio, writing about us in the papers.'

I look really smug in the picture too. People are going to hate us.

Tuesday 20 February

Lunch with Kris Thykier today. Kris is the MD at Freud Communications, one of the biggest PR companies around. He arrives at Chez Gérard with the last *Heat* in his sweaty palm. He looks angry.

'What the hell are you doing?'

Always a good start.

'What do you mean?'

'You've printed a picture of one of my clients' houses.'

He opens the magazine at a story about Geri Halliwell. There, clear as anything, is her house. There's no street name but the number of the house is clear.

'There's burglars in London right now targeting rich people. You can't do this.'

'But there's no street name on it! Kris, it'll be fine.'

Eventually he calms down. Of course it'll be fine. PR people worry too much.

Monday 26 February

Oh my God. Just got back from the Brit Awards and no one is talking about the performances or who won what. They're talking about Geri bloody Halliwell, who debuted her new body on the show. There's nothing of her! She looks like she's down to about seven stone, and she clearly wanted to show off all her hard work (short skirt, gold bra top, boots and nothing else) and it's the most gobsmacking transformation I've ever seen. I liked the chunky Geri – clearly Geri didn't!

Tuesday 27 February

Birchy rushes into the office first thing. 'Geri Halliwell! It's a cover, surely!' I love Birchy. He's as amused by the scandal, the weight loss, the weight gain and the who-said-what-to-whom as I am. He's right, of course. He's always right.

'We won't get an interview in time,' I tell him, 'if at all.'

'Doesn't matter!' he says without a second's hesitation. 'Put her on the cover anyway.'

So we have done. Our Fashion Editor Ellie is blown away by her new look – 'Is that really her?' she said to me when I show the pictures, '*the* Geri Halliwell?' and is given the piece to write. It's our girliest cover yet – unashamedly interested in one woman's body. It feels kind of voyeuristic – we analyse every sinew, every bump on her body. 'Geri's Amazing New Look!' reads the breathless coverline. 'New body, new hair – how did she do that?'

Wednesday 28 February
Spent today in Brighton at Zoë Ball's house.

In decades past, journalists and famous people would spend days together, sometimes weeks, to get a decent interview. They'd go round their houses, go on tour with them, ring them for follow-up chats after the main interview had been done. Hell, many of them even slept together. These days most famous people will give you an hour of their time for an interview (if you're lucky), and a small percentage (growing for *Heat* because our sales are getting pretty high) will give you a photoshoot. Zoë sees it the old-fashioned way, which is why I spent all day with her today.

I got off the train at Brighton station just after 11, met up with our photographer Paul Rider who drove his mini down from London for the occasion: a mini packed with cameras, photographic umbrella, various other photographic paraphernalia, plus an assistant, make-up artist and hair person. I squeezed into the back and we headed out of Brighton towards Hove and immediately got lost. So we rang Zoë (celebrities letting journalists have their phone number – there's something that doesn't happen very often), she passed the phone to Norman (aka Fatboy Slim aka Zoë's husband) and he gave us directions. Which was useful because we were hopelessly, pathetically lost …

I tell Norman where we are …

'You've gone too far! Turn around.'

'Okay, we're heading back to Brighton.'

'Can you see a sign on your right that says No Entry?'

'Er, yep.'

'That has a winding lane just beyond it?'

'Yessss.'

'Go down there.'

'There' is the most exclusive road on the Sussex coast. A row of eight huge beach-front houses, each with their own bit of beach. Paul

McCartney owns one, Nick Berry – possibly the biggest TV actor of the moment, thanks to his starring role in *Heartbeat* – another, and Norman and Zoë? Well, they own two. Of course.

'Okay, we're going down the lane now.'

'Now can you see a balding bloke waving manically at you?'

And there he was. Norman Cook, superstar DJ, one of the ten richest musicians of the last year, waving his long bronzed arms above his head.

We'd made it.

Norman helped us with our bags and walked us into the house to meet Zoë. Just two and a half months after giving birth to baby Woody she's in great shape and doesn't look that tired, a situation that may be helped by a woman called Jackie, Woody's nanny. Also present are Norman's gooey-eyed parents and two people known as 'The Dusters'. They wear matching outfits and carry about the business with all the zeal and purpose of someone involved in major renovation work. In actual fact all they're doing is dusting. They come to the house to do this twice a week, every week of the year. Life of a celebrity, eh? You can have dusters on the payroll and everything!

However, if any house in all of Christendom needed over 100 dusts a year it's this one. It's not just two houses stuck together: it's two big, wide houses stuck together – so corridors go from east to west and stretch as far as the eye can see.

I ask for a tour – as if I was going to take no for an answer. First stop, the staircase and the display of hundreds of acid-house smileys. Smileys on mugs, smiley badges, smiley stickers. Miles of smileys.

Zoë leads us upstairs. 'Do you want to see the bar?'

Sure, what visit to a person's house is complete without a visit to the bar?

This one is vast – as big as the main bar at your average village pub. It has a huge neon sign (that reads 'Norm's Bar'), real optics to get real measures and, naturally, a pole. A great big, slippery, glistening pole. For pole-dancing.

Next is the balcony, with giant hot tub. 'I'd suggest doing the inter-view in the hot tub,' says Zoë, completely seriously, 'but it's raining.'

I didn't get to see either Zoë and Norm's bedroom or Woody's but I did see the kitchen (reassuringly messy) and the bathrooms.

Which leaves just the beach. The private beach. There's no garden here but, frankly, when you have your own piece of Brighton beach (or rather two pieces of beach, one comes with each house after all) that really doesn't matter.

The tour over, we headed to the upstairs lounge for the interview. Zoë appreciates the sit down – she's adjusting to having a child around, is doing extensive press for her new show and has just got her period so the chance to relax and chat for an hour or so is perfect for her.

I love Zoë. As nice as many famous people are it's often a real battle to get to see the real them. Spend five minutes in Zoë Ball's company and you get to see the real her. She is a hyperactive bundle of insecurities and is constantly in a panic about a million different things: what people think of her, her figure, saying the wrong thing. The last one is fascinating: normally people who are worried about saying the wrong thing and upsetting people are insular and bland. Zoë just shoots her mouth off all the time. If she meets someone and they're an arsehole to her she'll tell you as soon as they're out of the door – forgetting for a second that you'll print it and that she'll have to work with them again at some point in the future. Get her on the subject of the Spice Girls, say, and she's scathing: she'll tell you about the time she interviewed them and how one of them threw completely uncalled-for diva strops. Then she'll wonder why that person is funny with her the next time they speak.

Anyway, today there's no stopping her: she doesn't give a damn about Billie and Chris Evans, thinks his behaviour towards Geri Halliwell was 'appalling' before saying that the only reason Geri Halliwell got the figure she had at the Brits is because she 'doesn't eat'.

She's candid beyond belief, even telling me the story of how she and Norman nearly had sex a few hours after the birth when she was still high on the epidural. 'He climbed into bed with me and we're like, "Oh my God, what are we doing?" – getting a bit amorous. Then the nurse came in and we were like teenage kids getting caught out.'

She's great copy, gossipy, indiscreet and just fun. I adore her. I ended up spending several hours with her and Norman and headed back to London exhilarated, having made my first ever famous friend. It'll be holidays to Ibiza and nights out clubbing at Ministry before I know it, guaranteed.

Monday 5 March

There's something about editing a magazine that turns mild-mannered individuals into rabidly competitive sub-humans. For the last few months we've made all the news in the world of publishing – because of our incredible rising sales, because we instigated the Liam/Robbie war and because it seems we now have a direct line to the Beckhams (we wish!) This week, though, someone is threatening our top-dog status and I don't like it one single bit. Conde Nast, the high-end home of classy mags like *Vogue* and *GQ*, are launching a new magazine called *Glamour*. Some of their team used to work here and we like them but its very existence bugs me. Jealously I know they'll steal loads of our limelight and probably some of our sales. Their big, hugely expensive launch party is tomorrow. I'm invited but I can't face it. Going will mean spending all night telling them through gritted teeth how great their magazine is, which isn't going to happen. My competitive spirit won't let me go. I'm afraid that, even worse, I just want to rain on their parade.

Opposite the party venue in Leicester Square is a vast disused club called Sound. The place is gutted these days but their focal point remains – a 30-foot high screen stuck to the front. I asked the marketing team how much it would cost to hire it for the night tomorrow, and it's dirt cheap! I've had an evil idea, but we needed to execute it quickly. We've found a designer with a free hour and set him to work ...

Tuesday 6 March

Tonight I spent the evening outside a party I was meant to be at, taking pictures of a 30-foot tall screen. *Glamour*'s USP is that it's handbag sized. The jury is out on whether this is a bold move or an expensive folly. We hired the screen and got an ad together – this week's *Heat* cover accompanied by the words 'Size Does Matter'.

It looks incredible. Every taxi arriving at the party pulls up in front of it – people point and laugh at the advert. I know it's petty but to me it's hilarious.

Sunday 18 March

The band formed by the TV show *Popstars* – Hear'say – go straight in at number one, with their first single 'Pure and Simple' selling more copies in one week than any other record. Weird.

Tuesday 20 March
Police say Geri Halliwell's home was burgled on Sunday night. She came back from holiday yesterday to discover that her place had been broken into, obscene messages had been daubed on her walls, milk and Ribena sprayed everwhere (!) and that stuff had been stolen.

I feel terrible. Even if this isn't our fault – and I maintain that we made sure Geri's address was unidentifiable when we ran the picture – some people will still blame us.

Thursday 29 March
Called Geri's PR team to request an interview.

Their response is pretty blunt: 'No way.'

I'm not surprised, but feign surprise anyway: 'What? Why?'

'You know why – you printed a photo of her front door in your magazine.'

'Aw, come on!'

'Mark, it's a no.'

Tuesday 10 April
The *Daily Mirror* are claiming that Chris Evans and Billie Piper are now engaged! The paper says he proposed in Paris last week (on 1 April in fact, Evans' 35th birthday). The couple are holed up in his holiday home in Portugal, so aren't commenting. What is it about famous people that they have to do everything on fast forward? It's great for us obviously (always something to report – never a dull day!) but what is it about them that makes them want to do everything so bloody quickly? Slow down!

Wednesday 11 April
Geri Halliwell's record company have announced the release date for her next single. Now they'll do it. Ring the PR.

'So, erm, there's a release date for the single now.'

'Mark, she won't do an interview with you.'

Can't some people just forgive and forget?

Monday 23 April

Here's a turn-up for the books – Geri's PR is now phoning *me*.

'You know you wanted an interview with Geri?'

'A-ha.'

'Would it be a cover?'

Celebrities. They'll do anything for a front cover. Even talk to the magazine that may have got them burgled.

We have our interview.

Wednesday 25 April

Today – at last – was Geri Halliwell interview day. A day I never thought would come. By rights she should hate us. But she does have a single to promote, she's desperate to match the Spice Girls and get to number one with her comeback solo single – a version of The Weather Girls' camp classic 'It's Raining Men' – and being on our cover the week of release will help hugely.

Geri's doing a day of foreign press at St Martins Lane Hotel in central London and has hired the suite on the top floor. Pristine, white and elegant, it's one of those suites that is so posh that you don't want to touch a thing for fear that it might break. I've always liked Geri: smart, quotable, a proper celebrity. And today – maybe cos she feels she needs to butter me up, maybe cos for some reason I've become strangely irresistible to women for the day – Geri likes me …

After waiting an hour, she walks into the suite wearing shades, dragging her shih-tzu dog Harry and trailed by her entourage.

I love entourages – they're hilarious. They're the things that keep famous people from experiencing the real world. The more you want to be kept away from normal people, the larger the entourage. Part protection, part ego, you can tell a lot about an entourage.

Geri's is bijou, but entertaining: first up is her female personal assistant/best friend who videos everything she says and does. Then there's her press officer, Simon. An affable chap who just wants everything to go smoothly but gets tetchy when things run late. He checks his watch a lot. Then there's her head of international press. As we're gatecrashing a day of overseas press she resents my presence and wants to whisk Geri away from me from the moment we meet. They can go and take a running jump as far as I'm concerned.

I've been kept waiting for an hour but she's worth the wait, and is flirty from the off ...

'So, you're the man from *Heat*,' she says. 'Well, I need to eat before the interview. If I don't eat now I'll have to eat you.'

She carries on like this throughout the entire interview: chastising me, touching my knee. I'm sure I'm being seduced into giving her a good write-up but she's good at it. And she's not finished yet ...

I ask for a quick photo with her and she dutifully stands at my side. She looks up to me and smiles.

'Hi.'

'Er, hi.'

'This could look a little weird.'

I peer down at her.

'Yes, well ...'

Geri Halliwell is making me stutter.

'You see we really need a photo, so ...'

The PR is still fiddling with the camera.

'You're really tall.'

'Er, yep.'

'How tall are you?' she whispers.

'Um, six foot five.'

'You'd be really good father material.'

I gulp.

The photo set-up looks ludicrous. She's five foot not-very-much and I'm six foot five. As the guy taking the picture gets his camera ready she looks up at me. 'This is going to look stupid,' she concludes. 'How about I sit on your shoulders?' And so she does. With PRs flapping around, journalists being kept waiting in a room, here I am standing in a suite at a London hotel with Britain's most talked-about pop star's thighs wrapped around my neck. Tough job this.

Sunday 6 May

The celebrity world is in shock – Chris Evans has married Billie. The wedding took place at the Little Church of the West in Las Vegas (Noel Gallagher and Meg Mathews got married there a few years ago). Weddings there cost about 65 dollars for the basic hire of the church but the happy couple seemed to have chosen the pricier package – it included a video of their day, ten glossy photographs, a bouquet of flowers for her and a buttonhole for him. The whole event was very dressed down, however. He wore striped trousers and a green shirt, she wore a white cotton blouse, pink sarong and – my favourite detail – flip-flops.

Told you it wouldn't last.

Friday 25 May

Big Brother 2 kicked off today with a new set of housemates going into the show. This lot seem even better than last year's: some of the personalities are quirkier, there's a greater chance of sparks. I particularly like the look of one girl called Helen Adams, a sweet dizzy Welsh girl with a smiley positive demeanour. The production team speak about her in glowing terms: she's so excited to be alive, never mind be on the biggest TV show in Britain.

The press team very kindly slipped us the photos of the contestants in advance – we got them emailed over this afternoon. We also got a really heavy contract where I have to promise that no one else will see the photos until the show airs. I ignore it and get everyone to gather around Clara's computer where we look at the pictures one by one. Anarchy. Every photo provokes a huge reaction.

First comes Paul: young, moderately good looking with spiky hair.

'Gay!' shouts Julian.

'Gay!' shouts Polly, our new recruit from *Elle* magazine. It's fair to say Polly feels liberated to be outside of fashion-mag land, a world she's been trying to escape from for months. (Paul isn't actually gay, I point out, but they're not listening.)

Next is Penny, a late-thirty-something English teacher

'Too old,' screams Polly. 'Next! Come on!'

Then there's Dean, a thirty-something guy from Birmingham.

'Too old!' shouts Polly again. If Polly had her way the maximum age limit of *Big Brother* contestants would be 19.

'Gay!' shouts Julian, for good measure. (Dean isn't gay either.)

'Gay and too old!' hollers Polly.

You get the idea. Sorry Channel 4. Will keep them to myself next time (yeah, right).

Wednesday 6 June

Gradually, week by week, we're becoming talked about. People like our sense of humour, the way we write about celebrities. Today saw a huge break-through in our profile – in the opening titles of her new cookery show Nigella Lawson reads *Heat* while lying on a sofa. The episode is all about 'Guilty Pleasures'. That's what we've become: a fun, entertaining way of spending the time. This five-second clip of Nigella flicking through our pages will do us so much good.

Friday 20 July

Big Brother is obsessing the office again. As amazing as the first series was, we didn't really see much in the way of romance. This year we have. Sweet Helen has paired up with Paul who, early in the series, managed to prise himself away from the clutches of English teacher Penny (who's persistence got her evicted early on). *Big Brother* has been canny – the other week they conspired to get Paul and Helen together for a date. There's only one problem – she has a boyfriend. The conversations between the two fledgling lovebirds are fascinating – she's hesitant around him because of the boyfriend, and he doesn't want to do anything that will get him beaten up when he leaves the house. Their conversations are full of sexual tension, guilt, tenderness and, at times, excruciating awkwardness. It's as complicated as any relationship being formed in a student bar or workplace or nightclub. It's real. These are normal people figuring out what they want, and both seem unaware of the cameras. Tonight, though, the romance ended when the two of them went up against each other in the public vote and Paul was evicted. Helen's tears, as she gazed out of the window in the direction Paul had left, were heartbreaking. (Memo to self: It is only a TV show, I repeat, it is only a TV show).

Friday 27 July

It's the final of *Big Brother* and I'm laid up in bed with a ridiculous virus. The finals are becoming such a big deal now they really should be declared national holidays. Davina McCall starts tonight's show by saying hello to everyone who's having a *Big Brother* party as they watch the show. The *Heat* team – as well as working terribly, terribly hard – have their own party in the office which involves each of them dressing up as a different housemate. Polly found a blonde wig and put on fake tan to become Helen. Dan wore a tight-fitting top and put on a ridiculous pout to be Josh, the house's campest contestant. Brian, a sweet-natured Ryanair Trolley Dolly, wins.

Monday 13 August

I'm out of the office for a couple of weeks redesigning the mag again. It's been more than a year since we overhauled *Heat* and it's looking a little tired already. It's fine for monthly magazines, they can go for years without changing a thing, but we do 52 of these a year so we need to keep things looking fresh. In my absence Dominic Smith is in charge. Unflappable and experienced, he is ruling the roost expertly. Dom rings first thing with an idea for next week's cover …

'Helen and Paul want to do an interview with us.'

Great! Well, do it. It will sell loads.

'They want paying. Their agents said so.'

I am utterly speechless. That sweet lovely couple, who lived ordinary lives and had ordinary jobs and just happened to end up in a house that's filmed for a TV show, have gone and got themselves *agents*. Not just any agents – but the same company that represents Davina and Dermot. And they want a few thousand quid for their first interview.

Both of them intend to give at least some of the money to charity but still! *Heat* don't pay people! It's a ridiculous idea. But we really want this cover. The idea of these people having advisors and PRs and people to do their dry cleaning seems ludicrous but that is what's happening now. It's partly our fault, of course – if we make it clear there's a demand for them, they'll charge. Julian is doing the deal tonight.

Wednesday 15 August

A crazy day. We did our Helen and Paul shoot this afternoon and we now know how big a deal all this *Big Brother* stuff really is.

We sent a car for them, which picked them both up from Paul's mum and dad's in Reading. Julian called me from the shoot just before Helen and Paul were due to arrive there.

'They've just called me from the car – they're being trailed by paparazzi photographers! I've told them to lie down with blankets over their heads and come out of the car separately.'

This is madness. This is what people do for Madonna!

Half an hour later I get another call. It's Julian again.

'They're here now but you'll never guess what's just happened! A photographer from the *News of the World* has just tried to break into the shoot. He shimmied up the drainpipe and tried to get in through the window.'

The team are loving this. We've gone through a long period of people not giving a damn about us, so to have this attention is fantastic.

Thursday 16 August

Our latest sales were announced today – we now sell over 235,000 copies a week.

Tuesday 11 September

It's not often that I go out to lunch but today I did. Paige (our Reviews Editor) and I went to the nearby Berners Hotel to catch up on various things. We got back a little after two and were surprised to see the entire team gathered round the small TV screen above the news desk. A plane had crashed into one of the two World Trade Center towers in downtown New York. Then a second crashes into the other.

It's truly shocking and we all feel numb. Rapidly I come to the conclusion every other boss in the world must be coming to. No work today. Not that there's anything to report. The news channels have switched to rolling footage from New York, the evening papers have nothing but World Trade Center stuff and, most noticeably, there are no pictures of celebrities coming through. All the New York agencies have dispatched their paparazzi photographers to the site – snappers used to getting snatched pictures of Sharon Stone getting her groceries are now taking pictures of grim desperation.

Wednesday 12 September

There are no DJs on the radio today. The papers have dropped their gossip pages. The world feels different to how it was 48 hours ago. And still no pictures.

At half 11 Clara calls me over. 'Britney pictures, just in.'

Great! Britney. Britney will always bail us out.

I virtually run over to Clara's desk to look at them. It's Britney, just off a plane at Sydney Airport, in pieces. 'Her brother's in New York – she hadn't managed to get hold of him when this was taken.'

Her brother is fine but she didn't know it at that moment. Intrusive? Undoubtedly. But we need to run *something*.

Thursday 13 September

Still no DJs, still no gossip pages, still no pictures. Added to that are a glut of media think pieces about the role of celebrity, post the World Trade Center disaster. In a nutshell they're saying we're finished, 'the new seriousness' post 9/11 means that no one will want celebrities any more, there's no room, these days, for that kind of trivial stuff they say. We've finished this week's magazine– there's an interview with Kylie that, in the absence of any news, has become our cover feature. Everyone's writing us off, the celebrity world is dead, apparently, and we've got nothing to put in the magazine. Just as we announce record figures, the whole thing looks like it's about to go into reverse. Next week we'll get early sales on this issue. Don't think I'll come in that day. The game's well and truly up.

Urgh! George Clooney grows 'tache

This week's hottest celebrity news

£1.45 (450ptas) 22 - 28 September 2001

he.at.

NOW WITH ADDED HOROSCOPES!

EXCLUSIVE!

BRIAN

At last – his first ever interview!

He talks about sex, money & life as a celebrity

Issue 135

Exclusive interview with the outspoken star

KYLIE

"I feel sorry for Posh"

● Her true feelings about Posh
● Her baby plans
● The boyfriend rumours

BEST & WORST
BUMS & TUMS 2001
...but who's this?

CHAPTER FOUR
Thank God for Kylie
September – December 2001

Tuesday 18 September

This morning, on my way into work through Celebrity Central, I did my usual routine. In fact, I've done this every Tuesday for a year and a half since I was put in charge of *Heat*. I walk down the road, over the train track, down the hill, over the zebra crossing, then past two newsagents', the one by the road and the one in the tube station. As I walk past newsagent number one my pace slows, I look over my left shoulder and glance at the row of newly released celebrity magazines. Then on to newsagent number two. Here I stop altogether, peering through the glass into the shop. I'm doing what I do every week: rating the opposition, seeing who's brought in what exclusive and checking out how good our cover looks on the news-stand. Most weeks I beam, proud of how good we've made ourselves look, smug that we've beaten our rivals to the big interview of the week again. Today, at newsagent one and again at newsagent two, I wince. Anything about celebrities seems inappropriate this week. We're surrounded by newspapers reporting the incredible stories of death or survival and, increasingly, of grief. Our 'happy happy' stance looks even weirder as in both newsagents' we're next to *Hello* magazine who have forgone their usual cover diet of royalty or bland – but glammed up – Hollywood movie stars for an image of the Twin Towers on fire. I stand at the second newsagent's for longer than I normally would and watch as customers come and go. There seem to be more than normal and, without exception, they walk past the papers and, without giving *Hello* a second glance, pick up either *Heat* or *OK* or *Now*. I watched for ten minutes. In my head everything about the world was changing – that's certainly what our critics were saying – but not much about these women seems to have changed. Although I'm sure they're truly shocked by what has happened, their concerns are clearly still the same: will they get to work on time? Will their money last until the next pay packet? It's just that now more than ever they needed entertainment, a diversion from the horrors of the latest news bulletin. They want something frivolous, something to lose themselves in, something glamorous. And, based on what I saw, today they want a celebrity magazine.

Friday 21 September
Louise came in this morning with some early figures.

'Kylie issue looks like it's going to be huge, one of the biggest sellers of the year.'

What is it about Kylie? For three decades now she's been providing people with frothy, diversionary entertainment. She's number one in both the singles and album charts ('Can't Get You Out Of My Head' is the pop record of the year) and now she's selling us huge numbers of magazines in a week when they shouldn't be selling at all. No one provides escapism quite like Kylie Minogue.

Thursday 27 September
To the Hard Rock Café for the launch of a new TV programme called *Pop Idol*. It's a reinvention of the classic music audition show and looks fantastic. At the launch they showed a video of some of the good auditionees and some of the crap ones. And then there's Gareth Gates. Gates is a young – very young – lad from Yorkshire with a chronic stammer. It takes him several attempts to get his name out when the judges ask him. But when he sings the stammer goes – he sings like an angel.

As we leave the launch there's considerable debate about what we've just seen. For me, it was uncomfortable viewing.

'I think that's cruel. He clearly has no chance of being a singer. He's too nervous to speak! It'll kill him, poor lad.'

Polly Hudson, Queen Of Strong Opinions, agrees.

'Yeah, it's not fair. Imagine him singing on a live show.'

Boyd thinks otherwise. 'But he's fine when he sings! And anyway, they'll look after him.'

'It's cruel though, isn't it?' I ask. 'Putting someone through something, on TV, that will cause them so much stress.'

We're all agreed it will be a huge success, though.

'I WANT TO KNOW WHAT WILL HAPPEN TO HIIIIIIM!' screams Polly at the Hyde Park Corner traffic.

Hooked. Already!

Sunday 14 October

Out shopping with Gaby at Brent Cross, I stop off at the local WHSmith, as is my Sunday tradition ...

'Can you never give it a rest?'

'Huh?'

'Newspapers! Magazines!'

'It's my job! If I read them all now, inside the shop, that means I won't have to buy them so they won't clutter up the flat.'

She seems quite happy with this option. WHSmith, here I come ...

Sara Cox, the Radio 1 breakfast show DJ, is on honeymoon with her new husband, a DJ called Jon Carter. Today, the *Sunday People* have run some pictures that invade her privacy to a ridiculous extent. The pictures show the couple in the grounds of their private villa in the Seychelles, getting in and out of their jacuzzi. In most of the shots the couple are naked, their genitals covered by the paper's art department (Sara is shown topless in several, however). It's really odd – the laws of privacy clearly state that you can't run photos taken on private property. It's a stupid, reckless move that is so obviously going to get them into trouble. I fold the paper up, put it back on the rack and wander off. 'Rather them than me,' I think, 'that's going to cause someone a load of hassle.'

Watching TV this evening and ... Good God, Darius is back! ITV have just shown him making it through to the next stage of *Pop Idol*. His performances are still corny but the rendition he gave of Seal's 'Future Love Paradise' in this weekend's show was too good to see him chucked out. He's got to be back on our cover next week: everyone loves an underdog and Darius is just so good at it!

Monday 15 October

Without fail a huge Sunday newspaper exclusive leads to *a lot* of activity in magazine land the next day. Not only are we talking obsessively about it (usually around the news desk, the central point of the office and manned by the loudest people in the building, Dan and Polly, who are more than happy to engage a crowd of people in conversation about the latest scandal) but also Monday morning is the time when picture agencies try and sell second rights to whatever was the big set from that weekend's papers. Obviously it's the Sara Cox pictures we're offered early this morning and obviously I turned them down. An hour later the phone rings. It's Sara Cox's gravel-voiced agent, Melanie Coupland. And she's livid.

'I've been told you're buying these photos.'

'Of course we're not. It's obvious to me and anyone who looks at them that they're a flagrant invasion of privacy.'

'So why the HELL are you running with them.'

I've never spoken to this woman in my life and now she's screaming down the phone at me, accusing me of lying.

'Melanie, we are *not* running these pictures!'

'I've got it on good authority that you are.'

Hard to know where to go with this one. I decide to go down the repetition road. With extra indignation thrown in for good measure.

'Well, we're not!'

Journalists are often kept away from agents and it often frustrates the hell out of us – PRs feel like go-betweens at times, and you feel that only the people closest to them (the agents) can provide you with the answers that you want. But today I'm pretty glad I don't have to speak to agents all the time.

After ten minutes I calm her down, but she still doesn't believe me. Back in the firing line, and I've done nothing to warrant it. Went home in a bad, bad mood.

Tuesday 23 October

Sales continue to boom post 9/11, the world of celebrity seems to be getting bigger than ever and (surprisingly to all of us, particularly Louise who *still* doesn't get the appeal of the show at all) anything to do with *Big Brother* is big business even though the show ended months ago. Notable, then, that in this boom time the editor of the *Daily Mirror*, Piers Morgan, takes to the stage at an event in Belfast this evening to bemoan the growing celeb culture. 'Is my journalistic career going to depend on whether I can persuade some halfwit from Wales called Helen to take my company's £250,000 and reveal in sizzlingly tedious details that she's even more stupid than we first feared?' Morgan goes on to say that celebrity culture is on the way out: 'I hear secretaries talking about anthrax and Al Qaeda, not *EastEnders*.' He's wrong, of course: they're talking about anthrax *and* *EastEnders*. But the newspapers moving back to the serious stuff is a) understandable, they are 'news'papers after all and b) brilliant for us. Leave Helen to us, Piers, we'll have your sales.

Wednesday 24 October

The legend that is Barbara Charone – all five foot nothing of PR expertise – hosted a dinner tonight for Cher. It was impeccable PR – Cher was taken round to meet everyone in the room, chat (she's a charmer, as happy to talk about you as she is herself) and have her picture taken with you. I found myself staring at her throughout our blissful three and a half minutes together – really staring, observing every line and dimple. And I'm glad I did because while doing so, I made a brilliant discovery: Cher has no philtrum! You know, the bit between the bottom of your nose and the middle of your top lip. The bit that goes in. Well, hers doesn't go in! All the surgery, you see! Rather than get a cab back to Celebrity Central I walk home, full of my brilliant journalistic discovery. Cher: no philtrum! I'll be dining out on this for months.

Thursday 25 October

'Let me get this right,' says Julie, 'you met Cher and you didn't ask her about Tom Cruise.'

'Or the surgery,' says Jo Carnegie.

No one in the office seems in the slightest bit interested that Cher doesn't have a philtrum.

They think I'm a rubbish journalist. They're probably quite right.

Tuesday 6 November

Sales are increasing but we're still not being talked about enough. There's an interview in this week's issue that may be about to change all of that.

Boyd has just interviewed Frank Skinner. The conversation got on to the subject of relationships – Frank has just split up with Caroline Feraday, his girlfriend of a year, and as Feraday was considerably younger than he was Boyd asks why he always seems to go out with much younger women.

'The thing is,' he replies, 'there aren't many good older properties on the market. All the good ones have been snapped up by the time they're 25. There are single women in their thirties knocking around but they're all rough as arseholes so they're not really on the list at the moment.'

Is he joking? Who knows? But the papers will love this.

Wednesday 7 November

The papers are full of the Frank Skinner story. It's a funny thing with comedians – they can say the most inappropriate, outrageous things onstage (and loads of them do) and get away with it, but in print it just doesn't wash. Why is that? Why is something regarded as inoffensive in one context but when said by the same person in a different one it's out of order? He's clearly joking here – well, at least I hope he is – but the papers (and especially the Wednesday columnists) don't get it at all.

Thursday 8 November

I love Elton John: funny, smart, mouthy. The perfect celebrity. And today we find out he reads *Heat*. Clara beckoned me over just before five. 'Mark, look at these. We're famous!' There, on the screen of her Mac, is Elton, coming out of a newsagent's in Chelsea. Just behind him is the poor unfortunate newsagent struggling to carry a huge plastic bag full of what must be 20 or 30 magazines. On top, visible through the plastic, is that week's *Heat*. An amazing moment that I mark in the only way you should mark a moment like this: I phoned my mum.

Friday 9 November

Our biggest mailbag so far. Well, I say mailbag – it's all emails these days. Anyway, the Frank Skinner interview is causing a rumpus and I'm really not surprised. As the average age of the *Heat* reader is 25 years old his comments about how 'all the good ones have been snapped up by the time they're 25' has really struck a nerve, never mind what he said about women over 30.

There's so many of them that we dedicated almost the entire letters page to him.

> *Excuse me, Mr Skinner, but I would just like to set the record straight for all those single women over 25. We are simply making sure we do not end up with a man as opinionated as you.*
> **Sam, by email**

and

> *Mr Skinner, next time you label someone as 'rough', I suggest you take a look in the mirror, you haddock!*
> **Jenny, by email**

and

> *Frank Skinner's autobiography is a great read. In it he says he could only pull ugly birds until he was famous. Well, I must be really ugly because I'm a big fan of his and have met him a few times and he didn't offer to sleep with me!*
> **Debbie, by email**

Monday 12 November

Some nice pictures of Ewan McGregor with his new baby arrive in the office. His PR, Ciara Parkes, hears we've got them and threatens that he will have nothing to do with us if we run them. We replied by offering to drop all shots that show the baby's face. This is pretty generous of us – we don't have to do this at all; in fact, most other publications wouldn't do it. The child would be unidentifiable and no one would have any need to be upset about anything. But they're not interested. They say they'll still have nothing to do with us even if we don't show the baby's face. That's a pretty hollow threat anyway – McGregor, in common with most film stars, has nothing to do with us anyway, never gives us interviews, never does anything with us. Also, they were walking down a public street where anyone could see them. It's become a case of 'Damned if you do, damned if you don't'. If we're not helping our case by hiding the baby's face then let's not hide it – they're being pretty confrontational about it, which helps me make my decision. I really don't appreciate it when people are like that with my team. I've decided to run the pictures. We'll go to press with them at the end of the week.

Tuesday 13 November

We're really overdoing the cute thing with Gareth Gates now. Today we ran pictures of him in his school classroom: chewing on his pencil, looking dreamily at the blackboard. This is extreme bias, but we don't care. None of the other contenders get a look in, we're Gareth obsessed!

I overhear the girls on the picture desk discuss him.

'Look at his spiky hair …'

'He's got such a sweet grin!'

'Oh, look at him there!'

Oh deary me.

Monday 19 November

At ten to seven this evening, just before leaving the office, I received a fax from Ciara Parkes. She was the one at the end of the phone asking us not run the pictures of Ewan McGregor and his new baby. She was the one who turned down our – completely fair – compromise of running the photos with the child's face obscured. Clearly aware her tactics hadn't worked and that we were running the photos anyway she decides to get in a pre-emptive strike. The fax – sent to several big newspapers and magazines – reads really oddly.

I am writing to you with a request. Recently my client, Ewan McGregor and his wife Eve, have had a second daughter who seems to have attracted a huge amount of attention from the paparazzi.

Ewan would like to take this opportunity to politely ask that while he realises that doing the job he has chosen will attract press attention, it is not something he wants for his children. In the past, generally the press have behaved responsibly but recent events have prompted him to reiterate his vehemence in his wish to protect his daughters from photographers.

I am writing to ask you to respect his and his family's wishes and not publish pictures of his children. There will be publications that will not adhere to this request and I would like to make it clear that those that don't will not be included in any promotional activity pertaining to any of Ewan's future films.

We would like to thank you for you [sic] *co-operation in advance,*
Ciara Parkes
Publicist to Ewan McGregor

What's the point? They've made their case, not been prepared to settle for our compromise and sent us this, knowing full well our magazine – with the pictures – will be on the news-stands of Britain in just a few hours' time. And, again, there's that hollow 'you won't get any interviews' bit. Why?

Tuesday 20 November
The issue goes on sale. All is calm. Weird.

Tuesday 27 November
More controversial pictures. Well, Chris Moyles thinks so. I've known Moyles for five years – at a previous magazine I made him one of our 'Faces Of '97' when he was just starting out. It was the first time he'd been written about in a high-profile publication and he was pretty grateful (although, in his modest way, he reckoned he thoroughly deserved the accolade and probably much more beside). Despite his cocky exterior Moyles is a lovely guy – funny, personable, close to his family (whom he worships), loyal to his friends and a real charmer. He never forgot his first mention and tries to plug my magazines whenever he can. Today, though, he thinks *Heat* has overstepped the mark. Moyles, overweight for much of his life, is on a serious health kick. He's hired a personal trainer and he's embarking on twice-weekly workout sessions. Only fair, then, that we print some pictures in today's magazine showing just how hard he works out – all the stretches, the ball-throwing ...

He is not happy. I tuned in to his radio show just after four to hear him gearing up for a rant.

'This week's *Heat* magazine – Jesus Christ! They decide to hide in some bushes, take photos of me and print them with the clever-arse headline "Chris Moyles does some exercise!"'

He's shouting now.

'Listen to this: "He went a bit red in the face but soon recovered and stepped up the pace again by throwing – and catching – a yellow ball." Think that's easy, do you? Well, you try it!'

My phone rings.

'Chris wants to speak to you on air.'

'Oh, great.'

'Stay there, he'll be with you in a minute.'

What do I do? Turn my phone off? Probably shouldn't piss him off even more. Why do I give my phone number to famous people? I skulk into the TV room, where we do all our phone interviews.

'Mark, you're on air in ten seconds.'

Suddenly I'm live to the nation.

'Oi, Frith! You think that's easy, you try it! This Thursday morning, you're coming with us.'

Oh, brilliant.

After another five minutes of barracking he plays a record and he's finished with me. His assistant comes on the line and tells me where to meet them. This is no joke. I've not run since school. I don't do exercise beyond the odd length at the swimming pool. I HAVE NOTHING TO WEAR!

I emerge from the TV room to huge cheers from the team.

Then I spend the next hour fielding email after email. Everyone listens to Chris Moyles, it seems. Mark Ellen, the launch editor of *Q* magazine and a *Heat* staffer from the dark days, is the first. 'Brilliant banter just then! Brilliant!'

Banter? He ripped the piss out of me for half an hour!

Then others arrive:

'You can't buy that kind of publicity,' said one.

'Everyone knows about *Heat* now,' said another.

'So many people will be buying the magazine next week to see how you get on!'

Wednesday 28 November

Usually, my last words to my team as I head out of the door for the evening are cheery ones. I'm a cheery soul, really. On a typical day it would be something like 'See you tomorrow!' or 'Watch yourself on that bike! There's some nutters out there!' Today it was less cheery. 'I want to die ... where do I get tracksuit bottoms from around here then?'

Ellie, fashion guru for all occasions, even this one, points me in the direction of a sports shop in Covent Garden. I buy running bottoms, tracksuit top and fetching (well, so I reckon) Fila hat. I look at myself in the mirror. I actually almost look the part. Which is a good job because I'm bringing a photographer with me tomorrow. This might not be a complete disaster.

Thursday 29 November

Up bright and early. The meeting place is handy for me – the top of Primrose Hill itself, slap bang in the middle of Celebrity Central. I arrive first. Within minutes Personal Trainer Janie is there. Then Moyles's producer Will. Then his sidekick Comedy Dave. Then Production Assistant Lizzie (in full make-up, because she knows she's going to have her photo taken). But no Moyles. We ring him. No answer. We ring him again. Still no answer. Someone is dispatched to his house nearby and they beat on the door for ten minutes. No answer. And so, bizarrely, his entire team work up a sweat for an hour round Primrose Hill minus the reason we're doing it in the first place. Chris Moyles – what a lightweight.

Friday 30 November

Summoned to the Radio 1 studios to go on Moyles's show. Feeling really smug.

'So where were you?'

'No one called me!'

'Yes we did!'

'Well ... hmph.'

He's sulking. He sulks even more when Personal Trainer Janie tells him – and the millions listening – that I was 'really good – real promise'.

Typically, though, I didn't have the last laugh. Unbeknownst to me Radio 1 had their own photographer hiding incognito in the bushes, just as we had done two weeks earlier, to take photos of me flailing around a park at eight in the morning. Game, set and match. But like the email said the other day, you can't buy publicity like this.

Monday 3 December

Today the shit hit the fan.

The new issue of *Arena* landed on my desk first thing. *Arena* is Emap's men's fashion magazine and since we bought it from another company three years ago it's struggled to get decent sales.

To combat this they've recently given the editor's job to Anthony Noguera, the former *FHM* editor. The success of *Heat* must be real competition and likely to grab the attention of the Emap top brass – 'not a real magazine', is what he apparently tells anyone who's prepared to listen. Up to now any dislike had been kept to himself or his inner circle, his editorial team and acolytes who worship the ground he walks on.

The cover star of his new issue is my good friend Ewan McGregor. Conducted just a couple of weeks ago – in the midst of the fuss about our photos – McGregor is damning about *Heat*, the paparazzi and the celebrity culture we're both part of. At one point – and here's something to show the relatives – he appears to wish me dead.

'I knew that *Heat* magazine had got photographs of me and my kids,' he says at one point in the printed interview, 'and even though I went to them personally – or as personally as I would go because I don't trust myself not to lose my rag – they published them anyway. I wonder how the editors of these pieces of shit will feel on their deathbeds that their only contribution to humanity is to steal other people's privacy. What arseholes!'

There it is, in black and white: 'those pieces of shit'.

Management go into meltdown. They confront Noguera about the article – he denies he saw it and promises them it went in unread by him. It's an appalling state of affairs. I considered resigning there and then, but if I do it will just look stroppy and it will be me that loses out. No job and with my magazine known as a 'piece of shit' as my epitaph.

Not a good day.

Tuesday 4 December

Met John Noel for lunch. Noel is the agent *du jour*. He's got Davina McCall on his books along with Dermot O'Leary – two of the hottest stars of the moment thanks to the mega success that is *Big Brother*. Noel is hugely important to us. If he likes us we get access to those two before anyone else. Or instead of anyone else. He also signs up loads of the *Big Brother* evictees, the lifeblood of the magazine this past summer (alongside Kylie and Posh Spice – who still sells for us no matter what we do on her, no matter how tenuous the story). So this is an important lunch. Katherine Lister, Noel's ultra-canny in-house PR, comes along too, as does Julian.

John guides us to our table, seating us by the window at not a very nice table, despite the fact that the restaurant is almost completely empty. Julian and I are left with a good view of a grotty piece of pavement. What the hell's going on? Noel seems distracted and starts looking at his watch all the time. It's thoroughly unnerving. We order the food but John's still distracted and quite frankly I begin to wonder why we were there at all. Then, out of the corner of my eye, I see a mad-looking bloke amble down the street. The kind of bloke you'd swerve to avoid. He has a neck brace and naff clothes and he heads straight for us. Oh, great. Why do I always get the nutter? He rushes over to the window by where we're sitting, stares at us, then starts licking the window. What the hell?

Oh, great, I thought, now he's coming in …

The guy walks through the door, grabs Katherine and starts snogging her and introduces himself to us as Avid Merrion, *Heat*'s number one fan. Then he goes. 'That's Leigh,' whispers Katherine, 'John's new signing.' What a weird bloke, I think to myself on the way back to the office. And how odd that he walked past when we were there. I say this to Julian.

'It was a set-up! Don't you realise!'

Julian Linley may well be my faithful deputy, but at times he really does despair.

'Don't you get it? He put us by the window, told that guy what time to walk past, got him to do his act … it was all a set-up so that we know who he is.'

Sometimes I can be really thick.

'Oh. Oh, right. Yeah, yeah, of course, I knew that.'

Monday 10 December

I've taken on a new PA, Sal. Today wasn't her finest day. Don't get me wrong, she's great – hard-working, affable, loves *Heat*. What she isn't good at, so I found out at 11.36 this morning, is knowing who anyone is in the world of magazines.

'Mark!' she shouts across the open plan office. 'It's Alison, Richard Desmond's PA. She wants you to come in and see him.'

She then gives me her best 'beats me' shrug. The rest of the team stared at me with open mouths.

How to explain Richard Desmond? Here goes: he's in his early fifties, got a taste for the world of magazines when he sold advertising after school. He then went on to publish the UK edition of *Penthouse* and eventually various other porn magazines (Desmond disputes the word porn, saying that porn is illegal, his magazines don't feature anything illegal and that what he publishes are 'adult' magazines). Anyway, he also owns several 'adult' TV channels (The Fantasy Channel, Red Hot) and the far more respectable *OK* magazine. *OK* is the Don of celebrity magazines, one of the most profitable – if not the most profitable – of all the magazines on the UK news-stands. And it's *OK* that he wants to meet with me about. On Thursday.

After I put down the phone I took Sal into the TV room, gradually getting known around the office as the telling-off room. Been rude to a PR on the phone? Let's go into the TV room. Failed to book enough freelancers so we're here until BLOODY TEN O'CLOCK THREE NIGHTS IN A ROW! The TV room, please.

So me and Sal have a little chat, in the TV room, about being discreet and stuff like that. She takes it very well.

'Oh God, I'm so sorry! I've never heard of him!'

'Sal … it's fine. You had no reason to have heard of him.'

'I know who he is now!'

'Good, good. Now, we're going to have a new system from now on. You get a call, you ring through to me, you tell me who it is and then I tell you whether I'll take it.'

'Cool … sorry.'

My mind's racing about Thursday, I'm not really listening to what she's saying.

'Sorry, say that again?'

'I was just saying that's cool. And that I'm sorry. Again.'
Silence.
'Mark?'
'Yeah.'
'You're not going to leave, are you?'
'Sal … I don't know.'

CHAPTER FIVE
Gareth's going to walk it
December 2001 – May 2002

Thursday 13 December

Someone attempting to poach you is supposed to be one of the pinnacles of your time in a profession. It's meant to put an extra spring in your step, make you think you're king of the world, a chance to lord it up over everyone else. Not me. It just makes me feel really guilty.

So, at 8.57 a.m. this morning, when I arrived at Ludgate House, 245 Blackfriars Road, the home of Express Newspapers (proprietor R. Desmond), why did I try and keep my head down so no one could see me? Why did I say the words 'Richard' and 'Desmond' to the receptionist as though I was some ventriloquist, muttering through clenched teeth?

Well, there's several reasons.

One: someone already has the job I was about to be interviewed for (that's quite a good first reason in my book).

Two: I could have been recognised by anyone (which will make the situation referred to in Reason One a whole load trickier).

Three: because Emap has stuck by me through thick and thin (more thin than thick in recent years, to be frank). I felt like I was betraying them by even being here. By entertaining the idea of working for another company.

Other than that ... bring it on!

So there I am: jacket collar up, leaning in towards the receptionist (who leans back with a totally reasonable 'what the hell are you *doing*, lanky boy' look on her face. I'm speaking to her through clenched teeth when Desmond himself walks through the door. Nervous though I am, I spring into Mr Operator mode.

'Richard!'

'Mark ...'

So there he was – taller than I expected, full of presence with an unwavering eye contact.

We walked over to the lifts – I'd always been told that he had his own private lift but today, at least, he was more than happy to use the regular one. We made small talk and went up to his floor where all hope of me going through this incognito failed – to get to his office we needed to leave the lift then walk through the offices housing one of his newspapers. There weren't loads of people in – or if they were they were in meetings – but there were enough. Everyone else would hide away the editor from the rival company who they were trying to poach; Desmond wanted to show me off.

His office is vast. A huge, long thing with views of the Thames, a seating area with table and chairs at one end, private office with computer and phone at the other. And in the middle, something I've never seen in any other company boss's office – a full drum kit. Desmond is a keen drummer, plays in a band at charity dos – and staff in adjacent offices regularly hear him bash the hell out of them during the working day.

We sit down. His butler arrives. He has his own butler.

'Tea, sir?'

'Lovely, thank you. Er, normal tea, please ... erm ... milk, no sugar.'

A butler. A proper butler in formal get-up with a silver tray. A butler who – according to legend – delivers a banana to Desmond twice a day, at 11 a.m. and 5 p.m. Twice a day he comes in, lifts up the lid of his silver salver and offers his boss one of his two daily bananas. Brilliant. *I* want a butler.

Then down to business, although business in the more informal area to the left of the drum kit. With us is Paul Ashford, a softly spoken guy known as Desmond's right-hand man and billed officially as his Editorial Director. This means he's the guy who acts as a go-between between Richard and the editorial teams. Although, as he was about to prove, Richard Desmond doesn't seem to need a go-between ...

'How can we improve *OK*, then?'

Here we go. How do I answer the question without giving away all my trade secrets, while at the same time at least showing some kind of interest?

'Well, erm, I think it's doing pretty well. I think you could make it a little newsier, though.'

'News doesn't work for *OK*, we've tried.'

I start burbling on about the need to 'own' the celebrity magazine market, shutting others out and spending whatever it takes to get a dominant position.

He seems impressed. The tea arrives. I reach over to pour mine and the butler stops me and I let him do the honours. I may have just offended the butler.

When he's left, Desmond leans in.

'What I want to know is this – what do we have to do to get you over here, how much will it cost us and how quickly can we do it.'

He leans back.

I stutter. Again.

'Well, erm, well … I think that's jumping the gun somewhat. I'll need to think about it.'

'Fine, you think. Take your time.'

He leans back and lights a cigar.

Right. So he wants me to think now!

'Richard, I'm sorry, I just can't give you an answer now. I need to think about it.'

He'd been charm personified to me – nothing like as scary as I thought. But, of course, that was because he wanted me to do the job, so, of course, he was going to be. I knew, deep down, that I didn't want it.

I told him I'd call tomorrow. I think he saw this as a brush-off but was still unfailingly polite as he walked me to the lift, back through the now packed (it's an hour later and the working day has properly begun) editorial office.

Walking through reception I became convinced I was being watched by Nic McCarthy, the current editor of *OK*. I couldn't be 100 per cent sure it was her and felt far too guilty to look back. Instead, as I did when I arrived, I pulled the collar of my jacket up to my chin and kept my head down.

Friday 14 December

Spent most of this morning plucking up the courage to call Desmond. By 11.30 I thought 'sod it' and went into the TV room to make the call, notes in front of me mapping what I was going to say.

✳ Was lovely to meet you.
✳ I'm happy where I am at the moment.
✳ I'll have to decline your very kind offer.

All bland stuff.

I pick up the phone and dial his PA Alison, hoping, praying that it goes to voicemail. One ring, two rings – she's about to answer, I can feel it – three rings – DON'T ANSWER THE PHONE! – a fourth, then Alison's voice asking me to leave a message. Thank you, I will.

Saturday 15 December
I tell friends about Thursday. They're incredulous I didn't ask about the wage. 'You idiot!' says one. 'It could have been double what you're earning.' I should've done, of course. I think turning down the job without asking about the money makes me sound principled. They think I'm a fool. But then it's not the first time.

Monday 17 December
I was a guest on *Liquid News* again tonight, with Jenny Éclair, the maverick comedienne. Tradition has it that the guests (tonight, that's just me and her) gather in the green room to be briefed by one of the production team, usually a lovely guy called Andrew. Mid-briefing, Éclair decides this is her opportunity to get changed for the show. So she does. As Andrew briefs us, she takes her top off in front of us, pulls on a glam new one and straightens it. In the fine tradition of awkward British males we carry on talking regardless. Then the jeans come off, revealing a pair of skimpy, black lace knickers. Andrew manfully carries on the briefing as Jenny stands up in front of us and eases herself into her leather trousers. So this is what they mean by the racy world of television?

Wednesday 23 January 2002
On *Liquid News* again tonight. The fans of the show are up in arms that I'm on so much – bombarding the BBC's message boards with complaints every time I'm announced! Sod 'em, I love it. And they pay me. Christopher, the show's presenter, did an interview today where as well as going on – at length – about his beloved *Eurovision*,